From the Highlands to the Sea

From the Highlands to the Sea
Exploring the wineries of Monterey County
by Casey Young

Published by:
Mountain Vines Publishing, LLC
Post Office Box 385
Aptos, CA 95001 USA

orders@mountainvinespub.com
www.mountainvinespub.com

Cover Design by Richard Curtis, Santa Cruz, CA

Printed in China

ISBN. print ed. 0–9741357–3–9
First printing   2005

Publisher's Cataloging–in–Publication
(Provided by Quality Books, Inc.)

Young, Casey, 1951–
   From the highlands to the sea : exploring the
wineries of Monterey County / by Casey Young ;
photographs by Ken Dawes ; foreword by Jerry Lohr.
   p. cm.
   Includes bibliographical references.
   LCCN 2004117413
   ISBN 0–9741357–3–9

   1. Wine and wine making   California   Monterey County.
2. Wineries   California   Monterey County   Guidebooks.
3. Monterey County (Calif.)   Guidebooks.   I. Title.

TP557.Y67 2005   663'.2'00979476
                        QBI04–200530

*This book is dedicated to the
Latino vineyard workers of the
Monterey County area.*

Acknowledgements

We'd like to acknowledge all of the winery owners, as well as vineyard and winery workers who create that delicious beverage known as wine. This book took far longer to produce than we had hoped and their patience with the process demonstrated their patience with wine creation.

Once again, Maggie Paul, our editor, finessed the words into pieces that bring alive the people we met. Pete Shanks, our copy editor, meticulously assured consistency and correctness.

Also, we'd like to thank all of you who read our first book and encouraged us to go forward with this next project.

Contents

Foreword

Monterey is a very special and unique place. Over the years, I have traveled quite extensively throughout the world's great tourism and agricultural regions, and none are as full of contrast as this wonderful stretch of California. To the west, the Monterey, Carmel, and Big Sur areas of Monterey County are certainly among the loveliest, most hospitable, historic and relaxing spots one can find anywhere. In the course of 50 years, I can count on the fingers of one hand the times when I haven't found the natural beauty and weather here exhilarating.

To the east, Monterey County is largely composed of the Salinas Valley with its hot days and extreme afternoon winds. In the valley, a perfect combination of soil and climate results in the most productive farmland I've ever seen. This area has always produced some of the finest food. Known first for its fruit and dairy, today Salinas yields the finest fresh vegetables of anywhere in the United States.

Now, as we enter the 21st century, Monterey produces some of the best-flavored wines as well. These wines add immeasurably to our enjoyment of Monterey County. Because Monterey winegrowing is so new, really only 40 years old, little has been written about all of the hardy folk (almost all of whom are still alive and very active) who continue to create the 'third leg' of this food, wine, and hospitality phenomenon, known as Monterey.

Casey Young and Ken Dawes have painstakingly sought out all of these passionate people, and distilled their essences into this handy book, which invites you to seek out these folks, and especially their wines. The publication of this book couldn't be more timely. Recently, renowned wine critic Robert Parker aptly wrote, "The Central Coast will rule America."[1] From the pioneering work of our winegrowers in adopting sustainable farming practices, to the distinctive and intense varietal flavor of Monterey wines, I think that evolution has begun.

Monterey County has two principal viticultural areas: Carmel Valley, just minutes from the Pacific Ocean, and the Salinas Valley, which parallels the coast 20 miles inland, where grapes are now being grown over an 80–mile stretch. For winemakers, the long, cool growing season and well-drained, gravelly and chalky loom soils make the grapes of Monterey ideal. For visitors, opportunities abound to explore the charm and character of this idyllic place. Whether in the valleys, the shops, or your favorite place to dine, you'll find the wines of Monterey well worth the search.

Jerry Lohr
J. Lohr Vineyards and Wines
December 2004

---

[1] Robert M. Parker, "Parker Predicts the Future," *Food and Wine*, October 2004.

Introduction

Before we began to do the research for this book, our knowledge of Monterey County was limited to a few trips to Monterey, Carmel-by-the-Sea, Carmel Valley and the view from Highway 101. What a difference a year makes!

In the past year we've observed the county through each season and from many different angles. We've explored the strange shapes of the Pinnacles and walked the Brosseau family vineyard on the Chalone bench land in the cool early morning. We've journeyed up and down the winding roads of Cachagua Canyon by Carmel Valley, experiencing wreath-making at Joullian and a wine club lunch with the Hellers. We've watched the valley change color as the sun set from the deck of the Hahn Estate/Smith & Hook tasting room. Every time we've traversed the Salinas Valley, we've witnessed the farm laborers planting, tending and harvesting the food we eat.

At each location we've been met by great hospitality. The Monterey County winery owners and winemakers understand that wine doesn't exist independently, but requires the accompaniment of great food and conversation to make it complete.

Explore these wineries — you'll be glad that you did!

Casey Young and Ken Dawes

The Land

The Monterey County landscape cannot be viewed as a whole. Wind, ocean and mountain ranges leave their marks, carving the land into diverse sections. Under the earth's surface, a history of continental shifts, raging rivers and inland seas have left the inland region with "Greenfield potatoes" (the local name for giant cobblestones) and half a volcano.

Within this varied terrain, the vineyard owners and winemakers determine where and how to grow their wine. Several distinct winemaking regions, otherwise known as American Viticultural Areas or AVAs, exist within the county: Carmel Valley, Santa Lucia Highlands, Chalone, Hames Valley, Arroyo Seco, San Bernabe, and San Lucas. The Monterey AVA encompasses these regions, as well as some surrounding land.[1]

Before Vineyards

Monterey County enjoys the coastal climate of California. The region is shaped by mountains which were raised from the sea several millennia ago, the rivers that tumbled much of the soil and rock into the Salinas Valley, and the coastal fog that either seeps into or roars up the valleys, depending on the wind and time of year.

Two of the tectonic plates that make up the earth's crust, the North American Plate and the Pacific Plate, collided about 250 million years ago; the Pacific Plate began to slide beneath the North American plate. Over the next 150 million years, it created the Klamath Mountains in northern California and the Peninsular Mountains in southern California. About 30 million years ago, the Pacific Plate started heading north in a jagged movement that still produces frequent earthquakes of varying sizes.

During this time, the Pacific Plate pushed up the edge of the North American Plate to form the California Transverse and Coastal Mountains. Both the Santa Lucia Mountains and the Gabilan Mountains are part of the larger Coastal Mountains. Because they were originally part of the ocean, marine deposits layer the Santa Lucia Mountains. In fact, according to Larry Gomez of Lockwood Vineyards, it's quite possible to find prehistoric sharks' teeth in the mountains. These marine deposits were brought down the slopes due to high levels of rain, eventually becoming shale within the Salinas Valley earth.

During this period, many volcanoes were created in southern California. One, a stratovolcano approximately 8,000 feet high and 25 miles long, was split during one of the many earthquakes caused by the shifting tectonic plates. Movements of the Pacific Plate brought the western half of the volcano 195 miles north to become part of the Gabilan Mountains. These pieces loom over the Chalone AVA as part of Pinnacles National Monument.

Rivers formed another significant feature of Monterey County. The 85-mile-long Salinas Valley was formed by the waters of the Salinas River as it flowed both above and below ground. The Salinas River, as well as other complex geological features, has created rich agricultural soil, allowing the valley to become a well-known agricultural region. In the year 2000 the book *Steinbeck Country Revisited* estimated the value of Salinas Valley agriculture at more than $2 billion annually.

Arroyo Seco River

The Arroyo Seco River spills out of the Santa Lucia Mountains near Soledad and Greenfield. Significantly smaller than its original size, the river formed bench lands and cliffs which protect much of this area from the constant wind. It also left behind river rocks, or cobblestones, that store and release heat, and provide drainage for crops. These stones have come to be known as 'Greenfield potatoes.'

Climatic Regions

The University of California (U.C.) Davis is well known for viticulture and enology, with a great deal of research devoted to these two fields. One area of research undertaken in 1944 was to identify climate characteristics for geographic regions of California as they apply to growing wine grapes. (Similar research had already been done for growing table and raisin grapes, but did not address the cultivation of wine grapes.) Based upon climatological data from the United States Weather Bureau stations, as well as the university, two professors at the university, Maynard Amertine and A.J. Winkler, devised a system of segregating the wine grape growing areas of California into five climatic regions. The most important determining factor in the professors' point of view was temperature.

Professors Amertine and Winkler measured temperature based on a formula that determined "heat summation" for a particular area. The formula summed the mean monthly temperature for the period they were analyzing. They concluded there were five different regions, with Region I having the coolest average temperature and Region V having the warmest.

The professors then made recommendations for the kind of varietal grapes that should be planted in each region. For example, Region I, they felt, was ideally suited for "early maturing premium-quality dry table wine varieties."[2] In the early 1960s, the professors named the Salinas and Carmel Valleys as Region I, II and III wine-grape growing areas.

The system of regions devised by the professors had enormous impact on the wine growing business. People planted according to the specifications laid out. Unfortunately, for many wine-growing areas, the information didn't take into account the variations (or microclimates) within a region.

The Salinas Valley's daily wind is a significant contributor to the climate. If you drive north along U.S. Highway 101 in the early afternoon, particularly in the summer, you will find your way impeded by a strong headwind. Salinas Valley residents note that you can almost set your clock to 2 p.m. when the wind starts. Instruments that measure the health and vigor of wine grapevines record a drop in leaf photosynthesis processing so that the vine can preserve its moisture. This leads to a slower ripening of grapes.

As more information about the various microclimates in the Salinas Valley has been revealed, the sub-AVAs within Monterey County have proliferated. Within the Salinas Valley, the southern third can be classified more as a Region III, an area where Cabernet Sauvignon grapes do grow well. The northern portion of the valley from the bay to the area around Gonzales is still denoted a Region I because it is close to the wind and fog of the Monterey Bay. The San Lucas area crosses over to a warm Region IV.

In their petition for their own AVA, the Carmel Valley petitioners stated, "Although Carmel Valley and nearby Salinas Valley are both Region I heat summation areas, the higher elevation in Carmel Valley curbs the marine fog incursion producing more sunny days in Carmel Valley than in Salinas Valley." The petition goes on to talk about rainfall and soil type, which also differentiate the valley from the rest of the surrounding Monterey AVA. This warmer climate gives the growers in this area the ability to successfully grow Cabernet Sauvignon, a grape that never completely ripens in the northern half of the Salinas Valley.

Microclimates and *Terroir*

Going beyond Winkler's and Amertine's region system, many people talk about microclimates and *terroir*. Microclimates are pockets of variation within a larger climate. *Terroir* is a notion of soil and essence that includes not only climate, but also soil quality, drainage, and the like.

Chalone area limestone

The types of grapes grown and the flavor they impart vary drastically across the entire Monterey County AVA. When visiting the wineries, or purchasing wine with any of the Monterey County designations, it's fun to develop an awareness of where the grapes are grown. Are they general Monterey County grapes — meaning they can be grown anywhere in the county? Do they come from the slightly narrower Monterey AVA? Or does the wine carry the limestone flintiness of a Chalone Chardonnay? Is it a vineyard-designate wine such as a Joullian Merlot? Or on the contrary, does the wine carry the Central Coast label, a 1.5 million acre AVA that stretches from San Francisco southward? As you explore, discover what suits your own palate best.

Living Together

Monterey County's diversity is both its charm and its dilemma. A tourist-rich seacoast leads to the golf courses and ranches of Carmel Valley, blends into the sparsely populated Gabilan and Santa Lucia Mountains, and contrasts with the agricultural regions of the Salinas Valley. Trying to come up with one development plan for the entire county has proved to be contentious.

Vineyards are essentially agricultural businesses. Many of the vineyard and winery owners within Monterey County come from generations of farming families, either locally or from other farming regions in the U.S., with a suspicion of non-agriculture influences. The outstanding beauty of the Monterey coastline has attracted outside attention from those who want to preserve the unique elements of Monterey, and to study and protect the Monterey Bay, a National Marine Life Sanctuary.

In 1999 the county began to develop a General Plan Update that would chart the course of Monterey development for the following 20 years. It would influence where houses could be built, vineyards developed, wineries and tasting rooms created. It could ease or make extremely difficult the development of restaurants and lodging in some areas of the county. The plan could conserve or rapidly decimate the water table in the Salinas Valley. As with every controversial matter, there are strong, defensible arguments on both sides of the issue.

However, in July 2004, the Monterey County Board of Supervisors abandoned the plan they'd spent five years and over $5 million developing in favor of starting from scratch. Several groups protested and formed the Coalition to Protect Housing, Farmland, Air and Water. As of this writing, the sentiments of people on both sides of the issue have hardened. Whatever the resolution, it will have an impact on the land and people of Monterey County.

Apparently absent from much of the discussion, although profoundly impacted by it, are many of the people who till the fields and tend the vines of Monterey County — the agricultural farm workers.

Traveling Through the Land

Many people view Monterey County as beginning at the Monterey Bay Aquarium and ending at the southern end of Highway 101. If you fall into this category, take time to get to know the county better.

Explore the great restaurants of Monterey and enjoy the tasting rooms that are developing in Cannery Row — Baywood Cellars and Taste of Monterey represent Monterey County. Many Santa Cruz Mountains wineries are also expanding to this location — including Clos La Chance, Silver Mountain and Bargetto. On your way to Carmel Valley, stop to visit Galante's new tasting room in Carmel-by-the-Sea. If you like cheese, The Cheese Shop in Carmel Plaza will satisfy your urge to try obscure cheeses from around the world. (Ask about their "love cheese.")

The beauty of exploring Carmel Valley Village's winery tasting rooms is that so many of them are located within walking distance of each other, although you will need to stop at Château Julien on the way up the valley road. You don't really see Carmel Valley until you explore beyond the village. Try hiking through Garland Ranch Regional Park. From some of the trails you can see Ingrid's Vineyard, owned by Bernardus and Robert Talbott's Diamond T Vineyard. Go to events at the wineries along Cachagua Road through the upper reaches of the Santa Lucia Mountains.

Moving from the bay to the Salinas Valley can take you to Ventana Vineyards tasting room next to Tarpy's restaurant a fun place for lunch. Both are on Highway 68 by the airport outside of Monterey.

To learn more about the agricultural history of the Salinas Valley, as well as re-acquaint yourself with John Steinbeck, visit the Steinbeck Museum in Salinas. Then stop at the Salinas branch of the Taste of Monterey next door, to explore more of Monterey County's wines. The small Mexican restaurant nearby has good food at good prices.

When traveling through the Salinas Valley to visit the wineries, you have several roads to choose from. The best approach is to explore different areas at different times of the year. Watch the crops rotate through the season, the dark blue-green of cabbage leaves next to the vibrant yellow-green of lettuce. One week the field is littered with the remains of the harvest, the next bare earth waits to be planted. Always, there are workers, usually Hispanic. Some labor with machines, but many still toil with hoes, walking back and forth between the crop rows.

The vineyards will delight you as well — from the stark brown of winter to the gentle yellow-green of bud break — one of the earliest in all of California. The tender shoots turn dark green, and buds become hard nuts of future grapes. Through all of this, there are people working pruning, trimming leaves and eventually harvesting before the cycle begins again.

River Road brings you along the Santa Lucia Highlands, home to the tasting rooms of Pessagno Winery, Pavona Wines, Hahn Estates/ Smith & Hook, and Paraiso Vineyards. San Saba is building along the road as well, and there are other tasting rooms in the planning stages. The views from Hahn Estates/Smith & Hook and Paraiso Vineyards stretch across the valley to the Gabilan Mountains for a glimpse of the Pinnacles.

It's worth the time in the spring or fall to spend a weekend in the Chalone area. In addition to the winery, the trails through the Pinnacles National Monument allow you to experience bizarre geology and perhaps catch a glimpse of a condor soaring high. The Inn at the Pinnacles gives you a restful place to spend the night, basking in quiet above the hustling, fog-filled valley.

If you must hasten down Highway 101, allow some time to stop at the three wineries along the route — Blackstone Winery, Scheid Vineyards and Caviglia Vineyards before leaving the county. And be sure to make plans to come back because you've just scratched the surface; there are acres of wilderness, world class square dancing, mission ruins and the echoes of John Steinbeck to experience. Not to mention that wonderful expression of earth and climate

---

[1] AVAs are explained further later in the chapter.
[2] p. 66, *General Viticulture*, Winkler et. al, 1962.

Diamond T Vineyard from Garland Ranch County Park

History

Early Days

The long county begins at the southern end of the Monterey Bay and follows the Salinas River south, accessible by land or sea. Beguiling in its beauty, the land has provided sustenance to animals and people from the days of the Native American to the present. Proximity to the sea also provided fish for food. The Native Americans numbered about 10,000 and were divided into about 40 tribes prior to Spanish occupation. Before the 1760s, they fished, hunted or gathered as the seasons allowed, unaware of the short Franciscan priest that would impact their lives before the end of the century.

The Spaniards made several forays north in the sixteenth century, finding, naming and mislaying the cape at the south end of what was to become Monterey Bay. In 1542, having found the cape once again, Juan Cabrillo, a Portuguese sailor from Spain, named the cape *Punta de Los Pinos*. A little over 50 years later, Sebastian Vizcaine rediscovered the area and went on a naming spree. The mountains became the Santa Lucia Mountains in honor of a saint's day feast; Monterey was named after a Gaspar de Zuniga y Acevedo, the Count of Monterey and the viceroy of New Spain. The Carmel River (Rio Carmelo) was named for the three Carmelite friars Vizcaine had on board.

Carmel Mission

The Spaniards didn't return for another 150 years. Meanwhile, Father Junipero Serra, a Franciscan friar, established the first Catholic mission in Alta California in San Diego in 1769. He hitched a ride on one of the sailing vessels in 1770 to establish the second mission, San Carlos Borromeo de Carmela in Monterey. After some disagreements with secular authorities, he moved the mission to present-day Carmel, relocating his Native American converts, including several teenage girls, away from the men at the new settlement.

Making several trips between Monterey and San Diego by foot, Serra founded five more missions in the Salinas Valley before dying of cancer in 1784. Establishment of these missions was designed to convert the Native Americans to the Catholic faith. Needing wine to celebrate the mass, vineyards were planted near the missions. The mission era lasted less than a half century before the missions were secularized by the Mexican government in 1834, the Mexicans having won their independence from Spain and acquiring the California territory in the process.

The Salinas and Carmel Valleys began to change under the new occupants of the land. After the Native Americans were virtually decimated by the mission system, cattle ranching became the primary focus of the new inhabitants. In 1858 Colonel Agoston Harazsthy reported that there were 50,000 vines in the county, but they had disappeared by the end of the century — victims of the wine glut at the end of the 1800s. With the exception of a small area in the Gabilan Mountains, 1,800 feet above the Salinas Valley floor, the vines would not return in any significant way until the 1960s.

Gabilan Experiment

Charles Tamm, a Burgundian native, may have been the first to plant grapevines on the Gabilan bench land, in 1919, but there's no evidence that he ever made wine from the grapes of those vines. A man by the name of Will Silvear planted the first vineyards on what was to become the Chalone property in 1923. He sold his Pinot noir, Pinot blanc, Chardonnay and Chenin blanc grapes to wineries such as the Wente Brothers in Livermore.

Although this vineyard is still in use today, it almost didn't make it. Silvear's vineyard went to Dr. Edward Liska and John Sigman after his death, but by the 1960s it was in bad shape. Silvear's vines had been inexpertly pruned by vineyard workers and the lack of water on the bench land had become critical. The 35 acres of vineyards only produced 16 tons of grapes in 1960, less than a half ton per acre. This was well below the norm of two tons per acre for "stressed" vineyards today.

Through the eight years that followed, the ownership of the little vineyard changed hands several times until Dick Graff entered the picture. By 1969 Graff had become the proud owner of a vineyard that had no reliable water source, no telephone, and no electricity. Nor did Graff have the finances to make any major changes to the status of his vineyard.

Meanwhile, changes were happening on the valley floor below and in neighboring Carmel Valley.

The Push from the Santa Clara Valley

In the 1880s, the Santa Clara Valley, now known as bustling Silicon Valley, was an area covered by fruit trees and vineyards. Many of the vineyards were pulled out during the wine glut of the late 1800s, and again as Prohibition loomed. However, once Prohibition ended, vineyards began to be planted and the Santa Clara Valley provided grapes to nearby wineries such as Mirassou and wineries in other locations, such as Wente in Livermore.

As time went by, industry started to compete with the fruit and vineyards. Ultimately agriculture lost with one of the last orchards destroyed in the late 1990s. Vineyards were displaced for the cement of computer-chip buildings. While there are still wineries within the valley — J. Lohr and La Rochelle (formerly Mirassou), for example — the vast acreages of vineyards are gone.

When this trend first became apparent in the 1960s, wineries began to look for other areas to source their grapes. U.C. Davis recommended that wineries look to the south of the burgeoning city of San Jose to avoid suburbia. Almaden Winery had already planted 1,250 acres in what was to become the San Lucas American Viticultural Area (AVA) in Monterey County in the 1950s. Paul Masson (owned by Seagrams at that time) and Wente (Livermore) followed in the 1960s.

As wineries from the Santa Clara region emigrated south, another trend caused huge tracts of vineyards to be planted in Monterey County. During the 1970s, tax laws made it advantageous for groups of investors to create agricultural partnerships. It was a profitable venture since planting vineyards could give up to 165% return on investment. Both these trends increased Monterey's vineyards from about 8,000 planted acres in 1960 to about 15,000 planted acres in the early 1970s. By 1975 there were 35,000 planted acres in Monterey County. But this was not sustainable growth.

Two major factors impacted the trend. The first was a change in the tax laws. The second was the poor reputation of the grapes that were planted. As Doug Meader pointed out, vines were planted where they shouldn't have been because the planters weren't farmers, they were tax avoiders. The other factor was the poor recommendations made by some U.C. Davis professors.[1]

Peter Mirassou noted another problem that early vineyard managers in Monterey faced. Because the land had been used for non-vineyard crops for many years, there was a high nitrogen carry-over in the fields. This caused the vine canes and leaves to be lush — a veritable jungle. The overgreening of the vine kept the fruit from intensifying. By developing an understanding of how to irrigate correctly for the land, Peter and other winemakers were able to control the vine output and achieve the results they wanted from the fruit. But this took several years.

The reputation of wines made from Monterey County grapes in the 1970s was generally poor. A common complaint was that they were too herbaceous. Consumers thought of Salinas lettuce while drinking Salinas wine.

Yet some of these early Monterey County companies survived and continue today. The owners figured out that U.C. Davis had been mistaken in some of their recommendations. Winegrowers discovered other parts of the valley that had different climate characteristics from the straight shot down Route 101. Others knew what they were doing from the beginning. They were called contrarians at the time, but history has proven them right.

Daniel, Jim and Peter Mirassou

It's difficult to talk about Monterey County winemakers without discussing the various types of winemaking establishments within the county. There is a huge range of winery sizes, ranging from those producing 350 cases per year to those producing one and a half million cases a year. Beyond these single-owner vineyards within the county, there are the wineries that own vineyards in Monterey County but produce their wine in places far from the county. These include the Hess Corporation, Wente and Mondavi, to name a few. A few of the Monterey County wineries, such as Scheid, produce wine to showcase their grapes, the bulk of which they sell to other wineries.

Finally there are those winemakers who might be referred to as *négociants* — a French term for wine merchants. In fact, if you look at a bottle of French wine, you can frequently find the term, indicating it was made by a person who purchased wine from more than one winery to produce the final product. In California, the term has expanded to include winemakers that buy bulk wine from other winemakers and bottle it under their own label. Some excellent wines are made this way, in spite of the bad reputation of bulk wine.

Large Wine Conglomerates

Several wineries and vineyards within Monterey County are owned by large conglomerates with headquarters outside of Monterey, or even California. These conglomerates have a fascinating, if convoluted, inter-relationship, which impacted Monterey County history.

Paul Masson was based in the Santa Cruz Mountains[2] before it was purchased by Seagram in 1943. Seagram was one of the oldest companies in the acquisitions business, beginning operations in Waterloo, Ontario, Canada in 1857. In 1961 Seagram, under the name of the Paul Masson winery, planted the first of its 4,500 acres in Monterey County near Greenfield and Soledad. It also created the large winery facility near Soledad. Seagram ultimately sold Paul Masson to Vintners International (part of Heublein) in 1987. The Monterey County facilities and land were subsequently broken in two and sold to Estancia Estates and Golden State Vintners.

Harvesting at night

In 1971 Heublein purchased United Vintners (Inglenook and Italian Swiss Colony). Almaden, which had planted vineyards in Monterey County in the 1950s, was purchased by Heublein in 1987, right before Heublein itself was acquired by RJR Nabisco.

In 1945 Mordecai Sands founded a small wine company called Canandaigua Wine in New York. His descendants started to expand his operation in the 1990s, acquiring several brands associated with Monterey. In 1994 they bought Almaden and Inglenook which controlled the Paul Masson brand. Canandaigua was purchased by Constellation Wines, which also owns Pacific Wine Partners (Blackstone Winery) and Franciscan Wines (Estancia Estates), among others.

The Golden State Vintners operation started with Arpaxat Setrakian and his family in the Central Valley in 1936. A large facility that uses part of the Paul Masson winery near Soledad, Golden State Vintners was purchased by The Wine Group, a former subsidiary of Coca-Cola, in 2004.

Wineries that Came and Went

As in many winemaking regions in California, wineries in Monterey County have come and gone. This is particularly true of wineries started in the 1970s.

The 9,600 acres of the Monterey Vineyard were planted by Myron McFarland, his brother, Gerald[3], and Dr. Richard Peterson from Beaulieu outside of Gonzales in 1973. A few years later Peterson and the McFarlands went separate ways. Another interested party in this particular winery was Gerald Asher, the wine writer, who was the marketing director. In 1977 the winery was sold to Coca Cola, subsequently to Seagram in 1983, and ultimately went out of business. One other person of note who was involved with this winery was Phil Franscioni, who was responsible for a lot of the winemaking throughout Monterey County during the early years of Monterey County winery expansion. Phil started as a winemaker for the Monterey Vineyard in 1986. Phil was also winemaker for the Tessara brand created in 1996.

The Monterey Peninsula Winery was founded by two dentists in 1974. Until 1986 they made wine in an old restaurant on the Monterey Salinas Highway. Then they moved their facilities to Sand City and lasted another ten years before selling to a wine group made up of former Heublein executives.

Deer Valley was also founded in 1974, with winemaker Ed Filice joining the company in 1977. After numerous changes in ownership, Deer Valley became part of Canandaigua. Ed Filice stayed on to develop the Mystic Cliffs brand for Canandaigua in 1998.

Several wineries appeared, but what happened to them is lost in mystery. For example, in 1984 the Crietzberg family started La Reina.

In 1997, Mildara Blass, Inc. was the first major Australian company to enter the California wine market with its own brand, Bayliss & Fortune. Recent information on this brand is also unavailable.

Monterey County American Viticultural Areas (AVAs)

Within Monterey County there are eight American Viticultural Areas (AVAs), seven of them sub-AVAs within the Monterey AVA. (An AVA is a government designation designed to identify grape growing regions with different soils and climates.) Monterey's 597,624 acres were established as an AVA in 1984. Monterey is part of the Central Coast AVA established in 1985. The Central Coast's roughly one and a half million acres are found in Alameda, Contra Costa, San Benito, San Francisco, San Luis Obispo, San Mateo, Santa Barbara, Santa Clara and Santa Cruz counties, as well as Monterey.

Chalone

In 1970 the Chalone Vineyard Corporation was created when Dick Graff was joined by John McQuown and W. Philip Woodward. The trio expanded the operation (still without electricity and telephone) and convinced the BATF to grant American Viticultural Area (AVA) status, the first in Monterey County, to the area in 1982, even though only one vineyard existed at the time.[4]

Others planted grapes on the bench lands in the 1980s; these were hardy souls willing to exist in the isolation that the area demanded. Michael Michaud, winemaker at Chalone until 1998, created his own vineyard. So did Richard Boer, the Chalone vineyard manager and the Brosseaus, weekenders who had fallen in love with the area after tasting a bottle of Chalone Chenin blanc. Dick Graff also had his own vineyard separate from the Chalone Vineyards endeavor.

In 1997 both Michael Michaud and Bill Brosseau started their own labels — Michaud Vineyard and Gabilan Cellars.

Carmel Valley

Carmel Valley winemaking primarily began with William Durney who planted red grape varietal vines in the first sizeable vineyard in Monterey County since the mission days, in the mountains surrounding Carmel Valley in 1968. In 1977 Durney began his winery with winemaker Miguel Martin. Although the winery was not financially successful, the wines were well respected. In 1989 Durney died and after struggling for a while to save the establishment, his widow sold the property to a group of European investors, led by Gilbert Heller. (Durney's cousin, Merv Griffin, still owns his vineyard near Carmel Valley.)

Winemakers in the Carmel Valley tend to create enterprises beyond winemaking, integrating a Provençal-like atmosphere into the small valley. In 1982 Robert and Patty Brower created a winery (Château Julien) in a French chateau style that graces the main road into the town, neatly symbolizing this connection. Walter Georis, a creative dynamo, started his vineyard in the Cachagua area of Carmel Valley in the same year, although he didn't release his first wine until 1984. Walter is also responsible for the Corkscrew restaurant and the newest art gallery in Carmel Village.

The Cachagua area of Carmel Valley became a vineyard gold mine during the 1980s. In addition to Durney's vineyard (now Heller Estate), the Joullian and Sias families purchased land for the Joullian vineyard in the same area in 1981. Robert Talbott also began his second vineyard and winery in Cachagua in 1983. Although the Galante family had owned ranch land in the area since 1969, it was in 1983 that they, too, began to expand beyond cattle and roses to create their own vineyard.

In 1981 several Carmel Valley vineyard owners petitioned for designation as an AVA. The BATF granted the petition in January 1983 for the 375 acres that comprise the region. The rough boundaries "run from the village of Carmel Valley southeasterly along the Carmel River and Cachagua Creek for a distance of approximately ten miles. The northeastern boundary is Tularcitos Ridge."[5] The southwest boundary is the Los Padres National Forest. The BATF states that the northwestern and southeastern boundaries are less well defined geographically. Since its establishment, the number of vineyards and wineries within the AVA has continued to grow, numbering approximately 13 new vineyards since 1983 on top of the seven already established.

Small "backyard" vineyards dot the Carmel Valley landscape. Bill Stahl, the owner of a Mercedes dealership in Monterey, planted vines to landscape his sister's home in the valley. He launched his own label, River Ranch, in 1987. Chateau Christina is also a backyard vineyard, started by Frank Joyce. Joyce planted vines in 1987 to insure that the hill behind his house was stabilized, and found joy in making his own wine in 1994.

In 1989, tired of dealing with twisting mountain roadways, Robert Talbott moved his winery to the Santa Lucia Highlands. His Cachagua winery was purchased by Bernardus Pon who, like the Hellers, brought a European flavor to the valley. One of the original Bernardus winemakers was Don Blackburn, who left to go to Byington in the Santa Cruz Mountains.[6] Bernardus also has a well-known lodge in the valley (Bernardus Lodge) completing the cycle of good food and wine within a small area.

In the 1990s, a second wave of Carmel Valley winemakers came on the scene. In 1993, a London banking group led by Gilbert Heller purchased the old Durney vineyard in Cachagua, turning it into a certified organic vineyard.

Three more small wineries came into existence at the end of the century. Bill Parsons (Parsonage) created his seven-acre vineyard just north of the village in 1997 and Paul Stokes and Lynn Sakasegawa (Wines of Carmel) planted their vineyard the same year. In 1998 the Heller tasting room operation moved from their location in Village Square in Carmel Valley to their present store on the main road. The owner of the Village Square property, Gary Sinnet, took advantage of the opportunity to start his own brand, Chateau Sinnet.

Arroyo Seco

The mouth of the Arroyo Seco River was one of the earliest areas planted in Monterey County. Livermore Valley's Wente Vineyards planted 700 acres in the area in 1963.

For the next decade the area was quiet, until other vineyard owners and wineries began to discover the richness that the area had to offer in regard to the quality of grapes produced. Doug Meader of Ventana began planting in this area in 1972. Scheid put part of their vast grape empire on this soil in the same year. Jerry Lohr also planted his Monterey acreage within the boundaries of what was to become the Arroyo Seco AVA.

In 1972 Bill and Gus Jekel planted their vineyards close to the mouth of the river. One of the more famous vineyards in the area was their Sanctuary Vineyard, full of huge cobblestones that came to be known as "Greenfield potatoes." The Jekels launched their winery in 1978. By the late 1980s they were ready to sell the winery and in 1990, Jekel briefly became part of the Vintech Group. When Vintech failed financially in 1991, the Jekels resumed ownership. They subsequently sold to the Brown-Forman organization (owners of Jack Daniels and Fetzer) in 1992. Brown-Forman closed Jekel in early 2004.

With over 32,000 acres (not all planted to vines), the Arroyo Seco AVA came into existence in 1983. It extends from the river's steep canyon at the western edge of the Salinas Valley and opens over the bench land to the Salinas River near Soledad and Greenfield. Kendall-Jackson and its subsidiary, Carmel Road, also have vineyards within the AVA which they began planting in 1982. Wente still maintains its vineyards, joined by other non-Monterey wineries like Mondavi.

For those with an adventurous streak, traveling through the Arroyo Seco canyon over the ridge to Carmel Valley is a beautiful, although slow, ride.

San Lucas

The San Lucas area in southern Monterey County was primarily ranch land during much of its post-Mexican existence. Almaden planted the first 1,250 acres within the area. Many of these vineyards are now held by some of the great vineyard management teams, such as Scheid. Some of the others no longer exist.

In 1981, the founding partners of Lockwood planted 1,670 acres in the area, starting the winery in 1989. In 1987, the BATF granted separate AVA status to the region, because its microclimate was significantly different from that of the rest of Monterey. However, in 2004, the Alcohol and Tobacco Tax and Trade Bureau (TTB), successor to BATF, removed 1,281 of the AVA's 35,362 acres to allot to the newest AVA in Monterey County — San Bernabe.

Santa Lucia Highlands

Just below the Santa Lucia Mountains, a folded area of bench land has been built up from the movement of land and water through the mountains over the centuries. Originally planted with row crops, the vineyard boom of the 1970s encouraged viticulturists to experiment with the climate of the Santa Lucia Highlands. What they found was that vineyards flourished — so much so that the region is gaining a unique reputation for its fruit. In the case of some vineyards, such as Pisoni and Garys' Vineyards, it translates to high prices for grapes.

Rich and Claudia Smith were among the first to plant in the Santa Lucia Highlands in 1973. Although they sell their grapes to many different wineries, they decided to create their own brand, Paraiso Vineyards (originally Paraiso Springs), in 1988. Further up River Road, Nicky Hahn purchased about 1,400 acres of cattle ranch in 1974 for the Hahn Estates/Smith & Hook Vineyards and Winery.

The next vineyard push for the area came in the late 1980s. Chuck Wagner (owner and winemaker of Caymus in Napa Valley) planted Chardonnay in the region in 1988. The first Mer Soleil Chardonnay was released in 1988. Four families started the Cloninger vineyard and winery in 1989. That winery closed in 2004 and, as of this writing, the facility is being leased by Steve Pessagno of Pessagno Vineyards. Pavona Winery, established in 1995, also has its tasting room on the premises. In 1989, Robert Talbott moved his winery from Carmel Valley to the Santa Lucia Highlands where he'd planted Chardonnay and Pinot noir. Talbott currently has 480 acres of vineyards in the Santa Lucia Highlands.

By the early 1990s there was enough evidence for the vineyard owners to petition for their own AVA; the petition was granted in 1992. The AVA covers 138 square miles of alluvial terraces on the west side of the Salinas River. It runs from Gonzales to the western edge of the Arroyo Seco AVA. Monterey County's 'wine corridor' runs along the eastern edge of this AVA. It provides stops at several wineries with tasting rooms (Pessagno Winery, Pavona Wines, Hahn Estates/Smith & Hook and Paraiso Vineyards). A few more tasting rooms, including Morgan Winery San Saba Vineyards, and Burnstein-Remark Winery, are in the planning stages.

The late 1990s brought several more vineyards to the area, including Morgan, Franscioni, Pisoni and Garys' Vineyards. Dan Lee of Morgan had been making wine since 1982 and was able to realize his dream of owning vineyard land in 1997. Gary Franscioni and Gary Pisoni came from local agricultural families and went to high school together in the Salinas Valley. They have their own individual vineyards (Franscioni's Rosella Vineyard and Pisoni Vineyard) and labels (Roar and Pisoni), as well as their combined vineyard, Garys' Vineyard.

Hames Valley

Vineyard owners in Monterey County grow primarily cool-weather grapes such as Pinot noir and Chardonnay. Tucked behind several ridges, the Hames Valley is freer of the daily wind that rushes down the Salinas Valley. Therefore, viticulturalists are able to grow warm-weather grapes, such as Cabernet Sauvignon.

Several vineyard management teams grow grapes in the valley, including Paraiso and Scheid. In 1988 the Denneys founded their ranch and vineyard in the valley. They began making wine in the 1990s, making them the only winery in the valley.

In April 1994, the BATF granted the 12,297 acres of Hames Valley AVA status.

San Bernabe

Almaden planted 2,000 acres of vines in this area in the 1970s. The company's plantings eventually became a 7,500 acre vineyard before becoming part of Prudential Insurance's investment in the area. The investment proved imprudent, and the vineyard was finally acquired by Delicato Family Vineyards, based in Manteca. Over the years, the size of the vineyard, like most in Monterey County, was reduced, but the 4,800 acre vineyard is still considered by some to be the largest contiguous vineyard in the world.

In 2004, the TTB granted the area its own unique AVA.

The Future

Although its winemaking history is short compared to much of California, Monterey County's wine acreage continues to grow, as do the quality and quantity of its wineries. The area is gaining in reputation throughout the wine world, particularly for its Chardonnay and Pinot noir.

Monterey County's wine future looks "rosé," indeed.

[1] See "The Land" for more information.
[2] See *Mountain Vines, Mountain Wines* for more information on Paul Masson.
[3] See Tudor Wines, page 109.
[4] See Chalone Vineyard, page 84.
[5] From the "Final Rule for the Establishment of Carmel Valley Viticultural Area"
[6] See *Mountain Vines, Mountain Wines.*

Acres of vineyards

The Wineries

The wineries are listed as they appear in the book. The number indicates the location of the winery within Monterey County on the map on the following page.

We have taken an inclusive view of Monterey wineries, including some because of historical interest (J. Lohr Vineyards and Wines and La Rochelle Winery), and some because they source their fruit from Monterey County (Banyan Wines).

The book is generally organized by AVA, starting from the north of Monterey County to the south. The two exceptions are the wineries of historical value (From the Beginning) and the Monterey AVA, which is at the end.

Plan your trip so you can take in wineries that are clustered together, such as a weekend in Carmel Village, or a day drive down River Road next to the Santa Lucia Highlands. Try to plan other activities with your wine tasting, such as hiking in the Pinnacles before visiting Chalone Vineyard. Above all, be safe and enjoy.

Pinnacles National Monument

The Wineries

From the Beginning
- J. Lohr Vineyards and Wines
- La Rochelle Winery

Carmel Valley
1. Bernardus Vineyards and Winery
2. Chateau Christina
3. Château Julien Wine Estate
4. Château Sinnet
5. Galante Vineyards
6. Georis Winery
7. Heller Estate
8. Joullian Vineyards
9. Parsonage Village Vineyard
10. River Ranch Vineyard
11. San Saba Vineyards
12. Talbott Vineyards
13. Wines of Carmel

Santa Lucia Highlands
14. Burnstein-Remark Winery
15. Hahn Estates/Smith & Hook
16. Morgan Winery
17. Paraiso Vineyards
18. Pavona Wines
19. Pessagno Winery
20. Pisoni Vineyards and Winery
21. Roar Wines

Arroyo Seco
22. Carmel Road Winery
23. Scheid Vineyards
24. Ventana Vineyards

San Bernabe
25. Delicato Vineyards

San Lucas
26. Lockwood Vineyard

Hames Valley
27. Hames Valley Vineyard

Chalone
28. Chalone Vineyard
29. Woodward/Graff Wine Foundation
30. Gabilan Cellars
31. Michaud Vineyard

Monterey County
- Banyan Wines
- Baywood Cellars
32. Blackstone Winery
33. Boyer Wines
- Carmichael Wine Company
34. Caviglia Vineyards
35. de Tierra Vineyards and Winery
36. Estancia Estates
37. Faun Vineyards
38. Golden State Vintners
39. McIntyre Vineyards
40. Parkfield Vineyard
41. Pelerin Wines
- Tudor Wines

Two of the early pioneers in Monterey County viticulture were the Mirassou family and Jerry Lohr. The Mirassou family now produces La Rochelle wine. Both wineries have tasting rooms open in San Jose. Because of their long association with Monterey County and their proximity to the area, we include them here.

Photo courtsey of E. & J. Gallo Winery

J. Lohr Vineyards and Wines

J. Lohr Vineyards and Wines

100 Lenzen Ave.
San Jose, CA 95126-2739
Phone: 408-288-5057
Fax: 408-993-2276
email: sjwinecenter@jlohr.com
Web site: www.jlohr.com
Annual Production: 800,000 cases
Winemaker: Jeff Meier
Winery Owners: Jerry Lohr and employees

Access
Open 10–5 daily except major holidays

Tastings
No tasting fee
Wines: Chardonnay, Riesling, Sauvignon blanc, Cabernet Sauvignon, Merlot, Pinot noir, Syrah, Shiraz, Zinfandel, White Zinfandel; J. Lohr Cuvée blends based on blending philosophies of selected Grand Cru wines; non-alcoholic wines

Sale of wine-related items? Yes

J. Lohr Wine Clubs
J. Lohr Wine Club: Six bottles four times a year for about $85 per shipment; other discounts, member-only events
J. Lohr Vineyards Select Wine Club: Four bottles twice a year at no more than $160 per shipment; other discounts, Vineyard Select member only events

Picnics and Programs
Participates in Monterey County Vintners and Growers Association events

Tucked into a lovely residential area of San Jose, you'll find the J. Lohr winery and tasting room. Although the facilities are located in San Jose, the emotional heart of this winery is in Monterey County.

Jerry Lohr grew up on a successful farm in northeastern South Dakota before leaving for graduate school at Stanford University in 1958. He ultimately received an M.S. and completed all course work for a Ph.D. in civil engineering before serving as a research scientist in the Air Force from 1961 to 1964. On his return, he began building his life's businesses.

Jerry started with a custom home-building business, partnering shortly after starting the company with Bernie Turgeon.[1] At about the same time, the pair became interested in the wine business. After studying the climate and soil of neighboring Monterey County, they purchased 280 acres near Greenfield in 1971. They planted vines over the next two years. Looking back over 30 years, Jerry claims that it was a really good decision, but not easy by any means. Monterey County provided a pretty hostile climate between the predictable winds of the Salinas Valley and the unpredictable winds of the county government.

Nonetheless, Jerry Lohr prevailed because he had a passion for wine and because he was committed to vertically integrated farming. This meant that he was in charge of the product from planting the vines, to making the wine, to marketing and distribution. He created a farming model that allowed him to retain control, sizing the vineyard and winery large enough to be viable yet small enough to keep a lid on capital investment for equipment. His vision also included an idea to produce wines in a style different from those made in California at the time.

Jerry began planting Cabernet Sauvignon, Merlot, Chardonnay and Riesling vines. However, he soon realized, along with many other Monterey County vineyard owners, that the information received from U.C. Davis regarding most appropriate varietal grapes for Salinas Valley was inaccurate. In 1978 he started grafting his fields to grow white varietal grapes (Chardonnay and Riesling) and one red varietal grape (Gamay). This decision has made it possible for Jerry to produce flavorful wine reflecting the moderately good soil (well drained, but not overly rich) and relatively cool climate of Monterey County. Jerry believes the area is too cool to properly ripen any red varietal grapes other than Pinot noir or Valdiguié (Gamay). On the other hand, Monterey County is

Jerry Lohr

J. Lohr tasting room

blessed with the earliest bud break of any wine-growing region in California, as well as a long, essentially rain-free autumn. This combination of climate and *terroir* gives depth and complexity to Chardonnay and makes Lohr's Valdiguié wines nearly unequaled in California. Jerry must be doing something right — his Riverstone Chardonnay has been the highest selling Chardonnay costing over $12 per bottle in the United States.

Jerry describes J. Lohr's winemaking style as very democratic (everyone's opinions are heard) with an eye towards making wines that are true to the flavor of a particular varietal. "It's important that each one of the wines be characteristic on a world basis for that wine in an optimum state," he says. A J. Lohr Chardonnay is characteristic of a Chardonnay grown in Monterey County *terroir*, yet not so out of character from a white Burgundy as to be unrecognizable. All J. Lohr wines come entirely from the Lohr vineyards.

Jerry's team works with both French and American oak barrels from several select coopers to achieve the desired aromas and palette-enriching flavors that enhance each wine's essence.

The bottling hall is compact, belying the large number of cases of wine that are bottled in the facility. J. Lohr is using screw caps on Cypress label wines. (Screw caps have started to become more popular in the last few years as winemakers searched for a way to cut down on the number of bottles which were 'corked' and subsequently ruined.) To Jerry, the screw cap is a wise decision for the Cypress wines because many of them are served by the glass in restaurants. The screw cap allows the wine to retain its flavor after being opened.

In 1974 Jerry bonded the winery, determining that San Jose was an easier place to establish his business, although remaining committed to Monterey County fruit for his white wines. Bernie retired from the winery in 1984. Jeff Meier, a U.C. Davis graduate, began working at J. Lohr during the 1984 harvest; in 1996, Jeff became the winemaker for J. Lohr.

There are many layers to J. Lohr wines — from the more expensive select vineyard wines to the well-recognized Estate series wines. At the end of the day, though, what Jerry Lohr wants is for his consumers to enjoy the experience enough to want to repeat it.

So, if you are in the neighborhood, stop by the winery to enjoy the wines of Monterey in San Jose.

---

[1] Bernie Turgeon is currently a partner in Trout Gulch Vineyards in the Santa Cruz Mountains. See *Mountain Vines, Mountain Wines.*

La Rochelle Winery

La Rochelle Winery

3000 Aborn Rd.
San Jose, CA 95135
Phone: 408-274-4000
Fax: 408-270-5881
email: dmuret@lrwine.com
Web site: www.lrwine.com
Annual Production: about 10,000 cases
Winemaker: Tom Stutz
Winery Owners: Mirassou family

Access
Open 12–5 Mon.–Sat.; 12–4 Sun.

Tastings
No tasting fee
Wines: Chardonnay, Pinot blanc, Merlot, Syrah, Zinfandel, Blanc de blanc (*méthode champenoise*)

Sale of wine-related items? Yes

Club La Rochelle
Shipments of two wines monthly at about $42 a shipment; events; additional discounts on wine and wine merchandise; red and white clubs available

Picnics and Programs
Private and corporate events in a variety of settings; picnic facilities available; participates in Monterey County Vintners and Growers Association events

Once upon a time, the Santa Clara Valley, now known as Silicon Valley, was covered with orchards and vineyards. In an eastern section of the valley, called Evergreen, Pierre Mirassou planted grapevines in 1854, creating a legacy that withstood the bulldozers of progress for generations. In the 1960s, his fifth-generation descendants, Jim,[1] Peter and Daniel, looked out over the valley and realized they were losing the race. Listening to advice from U.C. Davis's A.J. Winkler, they looked south to Monterey County for the acreage they needed to continue their family wine business.

Peter was in charge of creating new vineyards for the Mirassou family in Monterey County. While he was consulting for Almaden and Paul Masson wineries, he was involved with many other winegrowers who were also migrating to the Monterey area. The Salinas Valley had a lot to recommend it. There hadn't been vineyards in the valley during the phylloxera epidemic of the late 1800s; it had a good water supply without a significant rainfall; and it had areas where frost was unlikely. In November 1961 Peter moved his family to the Soledad area to manage the 275 acres of vineyard that the Mirassous had purchased.

Like many other vineyard pioneers in Monterey County, Peter learned, over time, the techniques that were best suited to the area. Vineyard planting narrowed from rows twelve feet across with vines every six or eight feet to rows ten feet across with vines every seven feet. Deficit irrigation was employed to counteract the high nitrogen level that existed due to the row crops that had previously occupied the land. The Cabernet Sauvignon grape was replaced by the more suitable Chardonnay grape. The change continues even now, as every few years a new block is replanted to keep up the production of the vineyard, and to add to the supply of grapes available for La Rochelle production.

The Mirassous coped with the daily winds by changing their farming. For example, they stopped irrigating their vineyard from the top, since it left a salt deposit which burnt the leaves when it dried. They adapted the mechanical harvester created by U.C. Davis in 1968 to insure that they could manage a timely harvest in Monterey as well as a winery in San Jose, and still create high quality wine.

In the 1960s, Monterey County welcomed the vineyard growers. Sugar beets and dry beans were subsidized crops in the valley and

Daniel and Peter Mirassou

vineyards were suited for soils that the row crop farmers didn't want — the well-drained soils of the bench lands on either side of the valley which were more beneficial for deep-rooted crops.

All the effort to understand Monterey County agriculture paid off, and still pays off in the production of La Rochelle wine. As growers like the Mirassous began to understand the plethora of microclimates that existed throughout Monterey County, they began to understand how the nuances of weather within each AVA influenced the flavor of a particular varietal grape. The Mirassous also understood the incredible climate variations within each vineyard, and put that knowledge to good use.

San Vincente, the original vineyard near Soledad, has gravelly soils. Since it is less foggy than the west side of the Salinas Valley, the Mirassous use it primarily for Chardonnay and Pinot noir grapes which they believe do well in these conditions. Pinot blanc grapes are planted within the Arroyo Seco AVA, which has richer soil and more fog. Pinot noir is also planted in the alluvial fan that slid off the mountains onto the Santa Lucia Highlands bench land.

The Mirassous farm their land with balance. They minimize the use of herbicides and pesticides, yet do what they need to do to keep their vineyards healthy. They focus on using Integrated Pest Management (IPM) to control pests in the most environmentally-friendly way possible.

La Rochelle relies upon 40 years of knowledge of growing vineyards in Monterey County to create their wines. Daniel talks about the appeal that a single vineyard within a single AVA with a single grower has for him. It makes the wine more exciting because the flavors of the *terroir* come through in each wine. Although La Rochelle produces 12–15 wines, they only have five or six varieties, including Chardonnay, Pinot blanc, Pinot noir, and Merlot. Cabernet Sauvignon and Zinfandel are produced when high-quality varietal grapes are available. This allows comparison and contrast of the essence of the vineyard within each varietal wine.

La Rochelle's uniqueness is based on Daniel's passion for the singular nature of the Mirassou vineyards. Since the wine is made by a single winemaker, Tom Stutz, the flavor of each particular place is captured in each bottle.

Entrance to La Rochelle Winery

The winery in Evergreen still stands, with a small vineyard around it. Wine continues to be made there, echoing the history of several generations. With the passing in 2004 of Jim Mirassou, Peter and Dan's brother, the family begins its evolution to another generation, with Mark, Peter's son, taking over the vineyard management in Monterey, and other members of the family participating in the business.

If you are in San Jose, take a trip out to Aborn Road to visit the tasting room. As you drive past a variety of strip malls, houses and restaurants, try to envision an earlier time when grapevines covered the land around you.

Carmel Valley

Slipping through the valley's neck . . . golf courses' brilliant green . . . whispers of vines' small spots . . . horses grazing . . . lodges and fine restaurants . . . the center of town . . . a jumble of small buildings . . . art lingering in secret places . . . tasting the wine . . . further out in the valley . . . road narrowing . . . mountains closing in . . . reopening to grazing land . . . up the winding roads to Cachagua . . . vineyards strung like hanging gardens on the mountains

Bernardus Winery and Vineyard

Mark Chesbro, winemaker at Bernardus, says, "Wine, from vineyard to glass, is really about people." He points out that the vineyard manager plays an important role in fruit cultivation, the harvest crew selects the grapes, and the cellar crew tends the fermenting juice. In fact, Mark includes the distribution channel and ultimate consumer in his viewpoint that the total wine experience necessitates considering the human aspect.

The Bernardus Winery and Vineyard, fifth in the Carmel Valley, was started by Bernardus (Ben) Pon. A native of the Netherlands, Pon's family owns the oldest wine distributor shop in Holland. Ben enjoys Bordeaux wines and believes that grapes from the Carmel Valley AVA produce the best Bordeaux-style wines in America.

The 220-acre estate in the Cachagua region of the Carmel Valley was planted with 50 acres of vines in 1990. Through the years the initial plantings of Cabernet Sauvignon, Cabernet Franc and Merlot have been enhanced with plantings of Petite Verdot and Sauvignon blanc. Recently, vineyard acreage has been increased to include a new vineyard in front of the Bernardus Lodge. This vineyard, named after Ben's wife, Ingrid, is planted to Chardonnay.

Todd Kenyon, vineyard manger for Bernardus, is a Carmel Valley native. He uses cover crops for organic fertilizer and beneficial insects to control pests, but doesn't neglect high tech. A radio-controlled hybrid watering system applies or withholds water in order to control vigor and fruit intensity.

When obtaining fruit from other vineyards for Bernardus wine, Mark looks for meticulous vineyard maintenance, rather than a particular style, such as organic farming. He says that the Salinas Valley is "mildew heaven," and withholding sulfur isn't an option for farmers who have thousands of dollars invested in long-term vineyards. Many of the grape growers within Monterey County are second- or third-generation farmers.

Mark came to the world of winemaking through a varied career of artisan cheese-making and heavy machinery operation. Wine was an everyday part of his family's life. While attending school in Europe, Mark's older brother learned about fermentation. He taught Mark about the process when Mark was 12, and Mark has been fermenting one thing or another ever since.

Attending U.C. Davis gave Mark the credentials he needed to become a winemaker, but with a family and a mortgage, he found that he couldn't afford the profession. So he worked crushing grapes during harvest when he wasn't running heavy equipment for his brother in Humboldt County. In 1989, he and his wife made the decision to move closer to her family in Southern California. They built a dairy from the ground up and made their entry into the artisan cheese world.

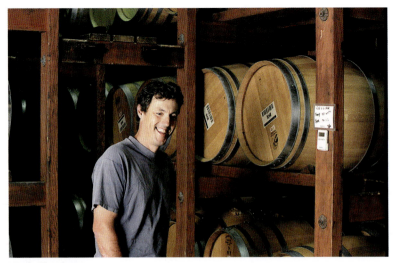

Mark Chesbro

After a year of working seven days a week, Mark gave up the idea, shut down the dairy and started to work at the Bernardus Winery — a mere five-minute drive from his home. He began with the harvest of 1994 and has never left, working every job from "cellar rat" to mechanic to chief enologist. In 1999 he was appointed to the winemaker position.

Red grapes coming into the winery are put through a crusher/de-stemmer and then barrel-fermented in French oak barrels. White grapes are crushed, but not de-stemmed before they are barrel-fermented. Mark does some experimentation with American oak barrels, and varies the coopers that he uses to achieve different flavors with the wine. He integrates barrels of different ages into the process to achieve the results he values. Thus, the reds are fermented in 50% new oak barrels, Chardonnay in one-third new oak barrels, and Sauvignon blanc is fermented in neutral oak barrels. (Neutral oak barrels are fairly old with very little oak flavor.) Mark feels that the fruit of the Sauvignon blanc grape can be overwhelmed with new oak which is why he uses the neutral barrels for fermentation for that varietal grape. To create Bernardus' Sauvignon blanc wine he adds some Semillon that has been aged in new oak barrels to add complexity to the blend.

In the last few years Mark has experimented with uninoculated fermentation for his white wines. In 2002, 25% of the whites went through this type of fermentation, which involves the use of native ("sticky") yeast rather than purchased yeast. Mark plans to use the process with 50% of the white fermentation in 2003. He finds that this method adds complexity to the aroma and "mouth feel" of the wine.

Bernardus Lodge and Ingrid's Vineyard

Mark believes he's able to handle the added complexity and work that using sticky yeast requires because of his excellent cellar crew. "Only those who are passionate about the wine industry work here," he says. It's a demanding job, he adds, but the cellar crew at Bernardus has a great deal of on-the-job training and recognition. Many leave the Bernardus cellar to study winemaking. While Mark regrets losing good workers, he is proud to have inspired their desire to learn more about the process.

According to Mark, the wine should say as much about where the grapes are grown, as the winemaker's skill. As you sip the wine in the Bernardus tasting room in Carmel Valley, remember all of the components — natural and human — which enhance your pleasure. Relish the beverage that celebrates Ben Pon's dream of the best Bordeaux in America.

Chateau Christina

60 Via Milpitas St.
Carmel Valley, CA 93924
Phone: 831-659-0312
Fax: 831-659-0312
Cell: 831-521-4319
email: joycevineyard@aol.com
Annual Production: 1000 cases
Winemaker: Frank Joyce
Winery Owner: Frank Joyce

Access
Winery:
1354 Dayton St. #6
Salinas, CA 93901
Open by appointment only

Tastings
Wines: Cabernet Sauvignon,
Merlot, Pinot noir, Syrah

Picnics and Programs
Participates in Monterey County
Vintners and Growers Association
and Carmel Valley Winegrowers
Association events

Frank Joyce loves being a dentist. He will never give it up. So what's he doing with two acres of grapes and a small winery?

The answer to the question begins with a steep hillside above the Joyce home in Carmel Valley. Frank's brother, Michael, a senior engineer, took one look at the house location and told Frank he needed to stabilize the hillside. If he didn't, the next El Nino–style rains would bury the house in a sea of mud. After debating the benefits of olive trees and vines, Frank chose the latter and planted vines in 1987. Michael's foresight became apparent in 1998, when a mudslide stopped at the upper edge of the vineyard.

When the vines were old enough to provide a decent yield, Frank discovered another benefit. Joe Davids, Dan Lee's assistant winemaker[1], declared that the fruit coming from the small plot was quite special — ideally reflecting the *terroir.* Frank had no trouble selling his fruit to other winemakers.

It's difficult to ignore the lure of ripening grapes in your own backyard — especially as you sink time and money into the project. Because of the slope of the vineyard, Frank can only farm it with animals or humans, a time-consuming and expensive endeavor, even with the help of his two sons, Michael and Russell. Eventually the song of ripening grapes became too great,

and with the help of Jim Clark, owner of the first cottage winery in Carmel Valley, Frank succumbed.

In 1994 Frank started making his home wine in his garage. He found that he enjoyed doing it and it didn't encroach too much on what he really loved to do — dentistry. However, Frank soon discovered that having a winery close by his home was not a particularly good thing. A detail-oriented man, Frank always found something to do in the winery. He discovered he was perpetually working and decided it wasn't beneficial. So, in 2001 he moved his winery to a small warehouse area in Salinas. The location is ideal — close enough to his dentist's office to be convenient — yet far enough away from the house to be inconvenient.

Frank has no set recipe for his winemaking; instead, he considers it an art. Every wine, every vintage is different. He concentrates on small lots of wine, doing everything by hand and using gravity to move the wine around — even when bottling. With his wine, as with his life, he tries to achieve balance.

Frank considers wine one of the true joys of living, as mystical a beverage as possible. As you enjoy good food, he hopes that you will enjoy the fine wines of Chateau Christina.

---

[1] See Morgan Winery, page 60.

Russell and Frank Joyce

Château Julien
Wine Estate

8940 Carmel Valley Rd.
Carmel, CA 92923
Phone: 831-624-2600
Fax: 831-624-6138
email: info@chateaujulien.com
Web site: www.chateaujulien.com
Annual Production: about
100,000 cases
Winemaker: Bill Anderson
Winery Owners: Bob and Patty
Brower

Access
Open 8–5 Mon–Fri.; 11–5 Sat.–
Sun.

Tastings
Tasting fee: $5
Wines by the glass available: $6
for private reserve; $5 for other
wines
Wines: Chardonnay, Sauvignon
blanc, Pinot grigio, Cabernet
Sauvignon, Merlot, Syrah,
Sangiovese, White Zinfandel

Sale of wine-related items? Yes

Wine Collector Program
Shipments of two wines every
other month at $35–$45 a
shipment; events; additional
discounts on wine and wine
merchandise

Picnics and Programs
Private and corporate events in
a variety of settings; group tours;
customized tours; picnic facilities
available; participates in Monterey
County Vintners and Growers
Association events

Château Julien Wine Estate

Bill Anderson, winemaker at Château Julien, compares himself to a master chef, adjusting acid, sugar and yeast (the spices of winemaking) in the frenzied period right after harvest. "To me," he says as he dashes from one part of the winery to another, "this is the best part of winemaking. Much of the rest of the year is spent coordinating people and numbers."

Bill has been with Château Julien since its inception in 1982. Bob and Patty Brower bonded the winery in 1981 and started building the château and producing wine in 1982. The name of the winery came from the St. Julien district in Bordeaux, and the lovely building on the 16-acre estate is a replica of a home on the French-Swiss border. Like many in the winemaking business, the couple was enchanted with the warmth and hospitality they found at the small château wineries of France, and they wanted to emulate that feeling in their Carmel Valley winery.

Paying attention to the vineyard is important for the Browers and Bill Anderson. Bill admits that good wine is born in the vineyard. His job is to facilitate the natural process, allowing the wine to evolve the way it wants, helping things along as needed.

Château Julien has two vineyards. The original six acres around the estate are planted with Sangiovese vines. In 1996 the winery owners planted 245 acres of vines in Lockwood Valley in the southern region of the Salinas Valley. These acres contain Chardonnay, Merlot, Cabernet Sauvignon, Sangiovese, Sauvignon blanc, Zinfandel, Syrah, Pinot grigio, Marsanne, Malbec, and Cabernet Franc grape varieties.

With these new vineyards, as well as purchased grapes, Château Julien creates wines made from 100 percent Monterey County grapes, although the vineyards they use come from several different AVAs within the county. All the grapes used in Château Julien wines benefit from the long Monterey County growing season, with the longer hang time providing richer fruit for the winemaker.

Bill Anderson got his start in the winemaking business at age 12. He'd heard that if you mixed fruit, yeast and sugar together, you could create wine. Armed with Fleishman's yeast, apricots and sugar, he fermented his first wine. Without having a full grasp of the process, however, he bottled while the wine was still fermenting and wound up with an apricot sparkling wine.

Bill's winemaking skills have since improved. After taking a slight detour to study psychology at Stanford, he re-embraced his love of math, mechanics and wine-making and the next thing he knew he was pursuing an enology degree at U.C. Davis.

A mixture of tinkerer and philosopher, Bill is fascinated by how things work. He extends this curiosity to people. Comparing human metabolism to that of wine fermentation, he says that the process of metabolizing sugar into energy is the same in both humans and wine. It's merely that wine goes an extra step beyond creating energy to create alcohol. "We're all a bunch of little fires," he says.

Harvest crush at Château Julien

He goes on to suggest that humans' close connection to wine is why we're so fascinated by it and the process of its creation. "Wine is a facilitator," Bill says. Along with water and food, it sets the stage for conversation, enabling person-to-person contact. Good wine does this effortlessly, stimulating conversation beyond one's immediate surroundings. Of course, Bill notes, bad wine does tend to break up a conversation.

Bill is a natural teacher. He so clearly loves his work that his enthusiasm for the process is contagious. Looking down into a 6,000-gallon stainless steel tank during pump-over, he claims the rich contrast of purple juice and pink froth is one of the prettiest sights of all.

Although Bill works closely with his associates Marta Kraftzeck and Ed Velazquez, he is ultimately responsible for the large number of tasks required right after harvest, from testing temperature and acid to mixing pounds of yeast and warm water to start the Chardonnay fermentation. If there are any mistakes, he says, he wants to be responsible for them rather than looking for someone else to blame. Of course, he adds with a grin, "If the wine is fabulous, I'm responsible for that, too."

Château Julien produces three brands: Château Julien, Garland Ranch, and Emerald Bay Coastal. The Château Julien brand breaks down further to Private Reserve, Estate Vineyard, and Barrel Selected labels. In a 2003 Château Julien newsletter, Bill Anderson states that his favorite wine is the Private Reserve Cabernet Sauvignon, but cautions that it should age about seven years before it's seriously tasted.

Each different brand has a different purpose. The Estate Vineyard showcases wines produced from the estate vineyard in Lockwood Valley, which had its first harvest in 1998. The Barrel Selected wines contain select Monterey County grapes, but they are designed to be drinkable shortly after they are purchased. Garland Ranch and Emerald Bay brands are geared towards national distribution, with the Emerald Bay brand containing more light and fruity wines.

A trip to the château provides you the opportunity to get away from the rat race. Unlike many wineries, there isn't a tasting bar; wines are graciously served from a long dark pine table in the great hall. Small group tours take you

Red wine pump-over

around the estate, from the breeze-filled patio area to the cool barrel-storage building called the Chai (pronounced shay). Events can be held in a variety of places around the estate — from the upstairs dining room, to the great hall, to the cobblestone garden courtyard, the conservatory, the cellar or the barrel building.

The visit allows you to taste the feeling of belonging to the Château Julien family. Bill Anderson finds it fascinating to be with this family of people who work closely together. Château Julien contributes to the community, he says, by providing both jobs and an environment where people can relax. The joy he finds in being part of this family comes from being involved in the "primary process of taking something straight from the ground, creating a finished product and watching everyone enjoy it."

So take a few moments out of your busy schedule and join the family at Château Julien.

Château Sinnet

Château Sinnet

13746 Center St.
Carmel, CA 93924
Phone: 831-659-0360
Fax: 831-659-2171
email: gary@chateausinnet.com
Web site:
www.chateausinnet.com
Annual Production: about 1,500 cases
Winemakers: Gary Sinnet and Bob Roudin
Winery Owner: Gary Sinnet

Access

Open 12–5 Sun., Mon., Thurs.;
12–6 Fri.–Sat.

Tastings

Tasting fee: $3
Wines: Chardonnay, Gewürztraminer, Cabernet Sauvignon, Merlot, Pinot noir, Syrah, Zinfandel, Claret (blend), sparkling, specialty and fruit wines

Sale of wine-related items? Yes

Gary Sinnet is a renaissance man whose interests include scuba diving, construction, travel, food, and, of course, wine. Like the man himself, Gary's entrance into the world of winemaking followed a path of his own making.

In the late 1980s, Gary developed a partnership with Gilbert Tortolani, of Gil's Gourmet Gallery, to develop such food and wine combinations as garlic-stuffed olives marinated in Chardonnay. Although the partnership itself is dissolved today, Gil continues to produce these olives with Château Sinnet Chardonnay. Recently, his garlic-stuffed olives won the award given by the American Tasting Institute for the best olive in North America.

It was also during the 1980s that Gary built several buildings in Carmel Valley Village in a complex known as Village Square/Carmel Valley Center. One of the buildings was occupied by the Durney Winery (which later became Heller Estates).[1] When Durney moved out in 1998, Gary realized that he could either use the space as a retail operation, or retain it as a tasting room. Since tasting room licenses were becoming harder to obtain in Carmel Valley, he decided to open his tasting room, and Château Sinnet was born.

To improve his knowledge of winemaking, Gary enlisted the help of Bob Roudon (one of the former owners of the Roudon-Smith Winery in the Santa Cruz Mountains) and read every book on the subject that he could find. In keeping with his life and hobbies, Sinnet wanted to have a range of varietal wines. He believes he has "the most extensive and diverse tasting in all of California." Since the tasting room offers about 17 different wines, including three different champagnes and three non-vinefera dessert wines, the claim has merit.

Gary maintains that there are two ways to begin a business: either wait until everything is ready or "open your door and let it happen." He's following the second method. As a result, there is continual change and growth at Château Sinnet and a constant challenge for Gary. Even something as routine as the purchase of foils for the tops of bottles can consume a lot more time than he'd like — in this particular case, 15 hours.

Three vineyards are used for the source of Château Sinnet wine: the Horned Toad in Cachagua, Busters (135 acres in King City) and a small vineyard in the center of Carmel Valley Village. The Carmel Valley vineyard is Gary's play area – he has 300 of nine varietal vines: Cabernet Sauvignon, Merlot, Pinot noir, Zinfandel, Touriga, Shiraz, Petite Syrah, and two different Chardonnays. He doesn't use chemicals, but isn't specifically organic. The vineyard rows, walked daily, have plastic owls to fight off the birds and gopher traps to capture the inevitable animals.

Gary Sinnet

Château Sinnet gift shop

The vineyard also contains a koi pond. Created in Château Sinnet's signature colors of purple and chartreuse, the pond is a Disneyland creation of flowing water, arched bridges and cement trees. Gary does everything with a sense of passion, and the koi pond is no exception.

Gary describes his tasting room as "the bar I always wanted to own." It is open longer than any other tasting room in Carmel Valley and also has one of the most eclectic gift shops, as Gary's interests are well reflected. A triangular wall rack contains 200–300 types of hot sauce. In addition to their potential heat, some of the brand names can bring a blush to the faint-hearted. This room, separate from the tasting bar, is crammed with other food items and serving dishes. Many of the food items are produced by Gil's Gourmet Gallery. For those with a sweet tooth, there are varieties of chocolate-covered fruits and caramels that magically find their way into your hands. Samples of these foods are provided along with the wine tastings.

A third room reflects Gary's incarnation as *Harold and his Purple Crayon* (a children's book). The room is filled with a variety of art memorabilia from numerous trips to Europe and Asia: Black Forest cuckoo clocks, large paintings, books, statues and more enhance the purple-walled room. Waterfalls trickle in the background and there's space for a band set-up, hinting at lively informal gatherings. A corner contains stacks of baskets, some packed with a combination of wine and foodstuffs. These represent Gary's commitment to the community — they are liberally handed out for auctions and giveaways when needed.

Gary Sinnet lives life to the fullest, yet understands the balance that he needs. High on the list are his wife, Joan, and his three children. The family participates in the winery business — Joan and Jessie work in the tasting room on busy days and Cory and Ryan help with the wine making and vineyard work. Everybody picks grapes.

Gary takes two months off a year to travel with one of his children. He glories in growing living things, as only a person born in the cement canyons of New York City can. Yet, he understands the rhythm of things, noting that "you can't be in a rush in the wine business. If you are, you're in the wrong business."

So make time out of your busy day to visit Château Sinnet and experience Gary's renaissance world.

[1] See Heller Estate, page 44.

Galante Vineyards

According to Jack Galante, owner of Galante Vineyards, "you should never follow good wine with water unless you're out of good wine." This is just one of the many cowboy philosophies that Jack espouses on a good day in the Cachagua Valley. Of course, he believes that most days in the valley are good days. "It's really part of old California," he says as he looks over the serene valley below him.

Jack's roots to old California stretch back to the beginning of the 20th century. His maternal great-grandfather, J.F. Devendorf, founded the town of Carmel-by-the-Sea in the early 1900s. Jack's father escaped fascist Italy in the 1940s. In 1969, Jack's parents purchased a 700-acre cattle ranch in the Cachagua Valley, although it wasn't until 1983 that they planted grapevines. With assistance from Greg Vita, winemaker with Jack, and Eliud Ortiz, vineyard manager, Jack started the winery in 1994.

Not pretentious, Jack determined that the winery be true to its roots as a cattle ranch. This philosophy permeates everything associated with the winery, from the hand-tooled leather labels on his three-liter bottles of Cabernet Sauvignon to the "wine gang" designation for the wine club.

The focus on a cowboy image doesn't keep Jack from concentrating on creating fine wines. Galante's single vineyard-designate Cabernet Sauvignon wines are 100 percent estate grown. The vineyards range in altitude from 850 to 1800 feet and are carefully tended by Ortiz. "Eliud does what he needs to do," Jack says. "He knows every plant. He reads the moon and knows exactly when the weather is going to change."

The vineyard is organically grown, with yields of about two tons an acre. No pesticides or herbicides are used and there is little irrigation. To determine when to pick, Greg tastes the grapes rather than relying on scientific analysis of acid and sugar levels. The grapes are crushed within an hour of harvest and then the winemakers work to let the grapes speak for themselves. Galante only pumps from the crusher/de-stemmer to the tanks, and uses gravity flow from that point on. Wine is aged in 100 percent French oak barrels and is neither filtered nor fined.

Many winemakers consider winemaking an extension of cooking and Jack is no exception. He's loved cooking since he was a child and continues to create new recipes and venues for cooking, including participating in a television cooking show. Guests can enjoy his efforts at the many events held at the vineyard, including the winery's *Annual Days of Wine and Roses* in September.

Not content with merely food and wine, Jack has progressed to pairing the perfect wine with movies. "You don't mix *Saving Private Ryan* with a Pinot grigio," he says, "You need a big Zinfandel."

The winery is a family affair and Jack's parents (who are in their 80s) remain active participants.

Jack Galante

Jack's two sons, Evan and John, also get involved in the ranching and winery. Jack's brother stops by on occasion from his home in Zimbabwe to lend a hand.

In 2004 Galante opened Carmel-by-the-Sea's first "Wine Tasting Room." The room embodies the western Galante theme. Hand-tooled leather abounds and guests have the opportunity to check out the cowhide-covered chair in the shape of a large cowboy boot. Galante decided to open the tasting room in Carmel-by-the-Sea to honor the role his great-grandfather played in the town's founding.

Jack Galante believes that one of the best reasons to know wine is to learn more about the geography and culture it represents. Wine is made in over 30 countries and represents not only the geography and culture, but also medicine, economics, art and more. Galante notes that in some way, wine relates to everything in our lives.

Although he acknowledges it is a tremendous amount of work, Jack Galante feels that wine truly reflects what life is all about — people's pleasure in meeting and greeting each other. He also feels that the perception many have of a winemaker's wealthy life-style is absolutely incorrect! In fact, according to Galante, dealing with the economics of a winery is perhaps the most difficult thing about the business. However, Jack doesn't let economics dictate how he makes his wine. He chooses quality over economics and will continue to let the Galante Vineyard speak for itself through the wine he makes.

When you have an afternoon to indulge in a scenic drive, beautiful view, great company and wine, make an appointment to visit Galante Vineyards. Or, if you find yourself in Carmel-By-The-Sea and want to have a glass of wine in relaxing surroundings, stop by the Galante tasting room. And remember, as Jack says, "Whether a glass is half empty or half full depends on if you're drinking or pouring!"

Galante tasting room

Georis Winery

Georis Winery

4 Pilot Rd.
Carmel Valley, CA 93924
Phone: 831-659-1050
Fax: 831-659-1054
Web site:
www.georiswine.com
Annual Production: 3,000 cases
Winemaker: Walter Georis
Winery Owner: Walter Georis

Access
Open 11–5 daily

Tastings
Tasting fee: $15–$20 depending
on choices (non-estate or estate
flight).
Wines: Sauvignon blanc,
Cabernet Sauvignon, Merlot,
Vincent (blend of Cabernet
Sauvignon and Merlot)

Sale of wine-related items? Yes

Georis Winery Wine Club
Shipment of two wines every other
month at $40–$60 plus shipping

Picnics and Programs
Participates in Carmel Valley
Winegrowers Association events

Even when he is sitting still, Walter Georis isn't really quiet. His eyes dart around and expressions flit across his face like clouds racing across the sky, reflecting his creative imagination. He is the owner of two restaurants and a winery, and he is also an artist, a musician, a designer, and a businessman, with pursuits too numerous to name.

Walter came to the United States from Belgium in 1956 when he was 11 years old. His family settled in San Clemente and opened a small ocean-front diner. Walter worked in the family business, but also pursued his interests in the arts and music. As a teen, he played guitar with his brother Gaston and friend John Blakely, in a surf band named the Sandals. A fortuitous encounter with Bruce Brown, an independent film maker led to the band's soundtrack for *The Endless Summer*.

Drawn to art, photography and design, Walter Georis pursued studies in these disciplines while living in Southern California. Later he abandoned that part of the state for the Central Coast, but still continued his artistic pursuits. Walter, like many artists, found it necessary to have a "day job." The job consisted of designing and creating leather handbags, which he sold in a small shop in Carmel. Walter expanded his inventory to include sandals by a little-known German company — Birkenstock. Because he sold so many of their sandals, the company asked him to design a marketing campaign for them. His ad was the key to launching the brand in the United States.

Not content with art, photography, design, marketing and music, Walter decided to open his own restaurant in Carmel in the mid-1970s. After meticulous design and construction in a southern French style, he opened Casanova in 1978. During the same time period, and spurred on by developing the restaurant's wine cellar, Georis began to seriously collect wine, particularly the Bordeaux varietal wines.

Walter is a man who follows his passions, and his passion for wine naturally segued into the idea of owning his own vineyard and winery. Not willing to begin without research, he made several trips to St. Émilion, France, to learn about the growing and winemaking methods that yielded the wine he liked. He discovered that the "old guys in France" had developed a wine-drinking clientele that understood the

Walter Georis

relationship of the underlying flavor of the wine to the soil in which the grapes were grown.

Walter's research led him to the belief that 40% of a wine's character comes from the land on which the grapes grow. Farming is the essence of winemaking, allowing the consumer to keep in touch with the grape's origins through the wine. The wine's flavor is a reflection of the soil and vineyard conditions.

In 1981 Walter Georis purchased land on Cachagua Road in upper Carmel Valley for his own vineyard. This land provides a common backbone to every wine that Georis has produced since 1984, the year of his first vintage. A Georis wine reflects the *terroir* nuances of the property. The changing years also show Walter's refined knowledge of his land, the varietal grapes that grow best in certain locations and the tending that each area requires.

The vineyard is also Georis's home, so he tends the land carefully, using as few chemicals as possible. His two teenage sons have planted their own half-acre vineyard and tried their hands at winemaking. Walter believes they are intuitive about the process, and have good palates as well.

Walter Georis is a strong and passionate man, one of varied interests and opinions. He has been a driving force behind the Carmel Valley Winemakers Association. Although he may not always agree with them, Walter honors his fellow winegrowers. They are like him, he says, having a sense of earth, climate, and seasons, yet realizing their own vulnerability as part of the human experience.

Walter Georis believes that Carmel Valley provides a well-balanced environment in which to live and work, allowing him to create a beautiful product that he can display in that setting. Wine, as a food, adds to the pleasure of living. In Carmel Valley, Walter believes, you can really live your life fully and understand why you're living it.

When you are in Carmel Valley, stop by the Corkscrew (Georis's Carmel Valley restaurant) and visit his nearby tasting room. There you can experience the eclectic tastes of the man, purchase a Sandals CD, and taste the reflection of the Carmel Valley land. A stroll through the small village brings you to art galleries that might be displaying Georis's paintings. The Carmel Valley Art Center is also a result of Walter's driving passion.

If you feel a strong presence near you in any of these places, look up and you may see the twinkle in the eye of a man who has always followed his dream and worked hard to make it come true.

Wagon and barrels outside the Georis tasting room

Heller Estate

Heller Estate

P.O. Box 999
Carmel, CA 92924
Phones: 800-625-VINO;
831-659-6220
Fax: 831-659-6226
email:
tastingroom@hellerestate.com
Web site: www.hellerestate.com
Annual Production: about 20,000 cases
Winemaker: Rich Tanguay
Winery Owners: Gilbert and Toby Heller

Access
Open 11–5 Mon.–Fri.; 11–6 Sat.–Sun.

Tastings
Tasting Room:
69 West Carmel Valley Rd.
Carmel, CA 92924
Tasting fee: $3
Wines: Chardonnay, Chenin blanc, Cuvée Gold (white blend), Merlot Rosé, Cabernet Franc, Cabernet Sauvignon, Merlot, Meritage; desert wines

Sale of wine-related items? Yes

Heller Estate Wine Clubs
Shipments of two to four wines four times a year at $49–$79 a shipment, depending on choice of clubs; events; additional discounts of wine and wine merchandise

Picnics and Programs
Picnic facilities available; participates in Monterey County Vintners and Growers Association and Carmel Valley Winegrowers Association events

It was the land that attracted the Hellers first. The steep peaks and sharp valleys of the Santa Lucia Mountains echoed the European mountains on their home continent. The vineyard, farmed organically from its inception, had been planted in 1968 by William Durney, one of the early pioneers of winemaking in Carmel Valley.

Toby and Gilbert Heller searched for vineyard property, primarily in Tuscany, but were put off by the chemicals that had been used in European vineyards. Pesticides accumulate in vineyard soil and plants. The Hellers felt it would take too long to convert these types of vineyards to the organic standard they were seeking. The Hellers are visionaries who know that the decisions they make and the footprints they leave will affect the world for generations to come.

Sculpture garden at Heller Estate tasting room

In 1993, a London banking group headed by Gilbert Heller purchased over 1,000 acres, the Durney's house and a chapel in the Cachagua region of Carmel Valley. There were over 100 acres of grape vines planted at an altitude of 1,200 to 1,500 feet in this location. After three years of "clean farming" (no herbicides or pesticides were used), the vineyard was certified organic. While the Hellers are very proud of what they've accomplished in the vineyard, they are also proud of their world class wines.

Rich Tanguay joined the Hellers as their winemaker in 2001. He got his start in the wine business by working in various wineries while pursuing a degree in Chemistry. He began his career in 1991 as a lab technician for Buena Vista (BV) where he learned aspects of chemical analysis, winemaking, cellar procedures and viticulture from such teachers as Jill Davis, along with Robert Stemmler, Anne Moller-Racke and André Tchelistcheff. In 1995, after a stint with William Hill, Tanguay became assistant winemaker at Buena Vista.

Just prior to moving to Heller Estate, Tanguay was assistant winemaker for Topolos in the Russian River Valley. It was at Topolos that Rick helped create wines from organically-produced grapes, similar to those he would work with at Heller Estate. Ten years of critical experience in organic farming prepared Rick for his position with Heller Estate.

Rich regards every wine as an expression of the vineyard during any given year; his desire is that you experience the character of the winery in each bottle. He refrains from manipulating the wine, even when he feels he could, allowing it to be what it wants to be.

Along with their winery, Toby Heller creates large sculptures and jewelry. Some of her work is displayed in a sculpture garden at the tasting room. The art that is represented on the Heller label is one of her designs. The original piece is a 15-foot-high bronze sculpture which dominates the vineyard view at the estate and represents the *joi de vivre* that emanates from the Hellers. The fine wines the Hellers produce reflect the dedication, devotion and drive that they have put into these unique, certified organic vineyards high in the Santa Lucia Mountains.

Toby and Gilbert Heller

Joullian Vineyards

Joullian Vineyards

P.O. Box 1400
Carmel Valley, CA 93924
Phone: 831-659-2800
Fax: 831-659-2802
email: information@joullian.com
Web site: www.joullian.com
Annual Production: 12,000 cases
Winemaker: Raymond (Ridge) Watson
Winery Owners: Jeannette Joullian-Sias and Dick Sias

Access
Tasting Room:
2 Village Dr. Suite A
Carmel Valley, CA 93924
Phone: 831-659-8100; 866-659-8101
Fax: 831-659-8102
Open 11–5 except major holidays

Tastings
Tasting fee: $3, refundable with purchase
Wines: Chardonnay, Sauvignon blanc, Cabernet Sauvignon, Merlot, Zinfandel
Syrah

Sale of wine-related items? Yes

Joullian's Inner Circle Wine Club
Two bottles four times a year for about $50 per shipment; member-only events

Picnics and Programs
Holds various events throughout the year; participates in Monterey County Vintners and Growers Association, and Carmel Valley Winegrowers Association events

At the southeastern end of the Carmel Valley AVA, along Cachagua Road, 40 acres of rolling vineyard blanket the shoulders of the Santa Lucia Mountains at 1400 feet. The vineyard is part of 655 acres purchased by the Joullian and Sias families of Oklahoma City, Oklahoma, in 1981. Their aim was to produce estate-crafted wines comparable to the finest wines of the world.

About fifteen years earlier, Ridge Watson was attending Stanford, living in a fraternity house and hosting tastings featuring vintners such as Michael Mondavi and Dan Mirassou. With a group like that, it was almost natural that there was a 450-bottle wine cellar in the house.

Following a short stint in the Peace Corps and a foray of five years into the retail business, Ridge followed his passion and achieved a degree in winemaking at Fresno State in 1980. He extended his training by working in Bordeaux (Château Carbonniex) and Australia (Hunter and Barossa Valleys). It was while he was in Australia that he received a call to join the Sias and Joullian families on their hunt to find the right land for Bordeaux varietals. Once the Carmel Valley property was found, the families worked hard to insure that they had the foundation to produce the wines they wanted.

The first challenge was to contour and terrace the rocky Arroyo Seco series loam into a property that could handle high-density-spaced vines. Two-thirds of the vineyard is planted to the Bordeaux varieties of Cabernet Sauvignon, Merlot, Cabernet Franc, Sauvignon blanc and Semillon. The remainder was originally Chardonnay, but it was grafted over to Zinfandel in the 1990s, in an effort to produce a Zinfandel that was structurally different from the over-extracted, ultra-ripe style currently in vogue with California winemakers.

Because he admired the vineyard of Château Margeaux, Ridge was committed to insuring that all of his vines were virus free. In 1983, while the contouring and terracing took place, Ridge made cuttings from California's finest virus-free vineyards and tended them in the nursery until they were ready to plant in 1984. Ridge recalls that they planted within 14 days, finishing on his birthday — a day he remembers exclusively for the accomplishment.

Joullian Vineyards has put all this effort into the land because they believe that "farming is the heart of making good wine." Although not certified organic, the vineyard is completely sustainable. The care of the land reflects the philosophy of many of the Carmel Valley winery owners. Carmel Valley wines are produced by people who farm and farm grapes to make classic wines, not as a "flavor of the month."

Ridge Watson

Prior to the completion of the well-engineered winery in 1990, Joullian wines were made at a custom-crush facility for two to three years. Controlling every process of the winemaking, from vineyard to bottle, is important to Ridge. The design of the winery allows Watson "to handle each vineyard block separately to insure that the complex subtleties and nuances produced in the field can be transferred into the bottle."

Joullian selects French coopers that age the wood three years before making barrels, believing that this technique provides much silkier and textured wines. They use barrels for an average of four years. Given the pressure of the Euro on prices in 2004, driving up the price of a new barrel by over $800, Ridge is concerned about the impact on the cost of the wine he produces.

Because they put so much effort into the vineyard, the Sias family feels that Joullian wine is expressive of the grapes and the *terroir* in which they're grown. Joullian wines are created more in the European style of winemaking, with an emphasis on balance and structure. The Siases feel that the consumer market is definitely moving in the direction of an elegantly balanced type of wine, and away from what Watson refers to as "the fruit bomb."

Because the winery itself is in the mountains far away from the center of Carmel Valley, Joullian operates a tasting room in Carmel Village. The building that houses the tasting room is a lovely stone building just off Carmel Valley Road in Carmel Valley Village. There are also events at the winery, some exclusive to wine club members, but some, like the annual open house, "Wine and Wreaths," are open to everyone. There you can make your own wreath from grape vines, eat well, drink fine Joullian wines and explore the vineyards and winery, often with Ridge as your guide. Listening to Ridge Watson talk passionately about viticulture, winemaking and the wines Joullian produces is an enthralling experience. If you get the chance, be sure to take advantage of it.

If you can't, stop by the tasting room and enjoy how the *terroir* of the grape, combined with the winemaker's knowledge and the Sias family's commitment, emerges

Joullian Vineyard

Parsonage Village Vineyard

P.O. Box 25
Carmel, CA 93924
Phone: 831-659-2215
Fax: 831-659-2215
email: info@parsonagewine.com
Web site:
www.parsonagewine.com
Annual Production: 1,500 cases
Winemaker: Bill Parsons
Winery Owners: Bill and Mary
Ellen Parsons

Access
Open by appointment

Tastings
Wines: Cabernet Sauvignon,
Merlot, Syrah

Sale of wine-related items? No

Picnics and Programs
Participates in Carmel Valley
Winegrowers Association events

Parsonage Village Vineyard

Bill Parsons enjoys his vineyard and winery because it "provides a relationship with nature that I wouldn't otherwise have." He goes on to describe a ghastly noise he heard one day as he was tending his vines. When he tracked down the sound, he saw a golden eagle struggling to lift a giant snake high enough to get away from a flock of crows that were attacking the eagle. Finally, the eagle dropped the snake to get away from the crows. The eagle's loss saddened Bill, because the bird had worked hard to get his meal and deserved to eat it — rather than being harassed by a flock of scavengers.

The story is also a metaphor for Bill and his wines. He and his wife, Mary, purchased nine and a quarter acres just outside the Carmel Valley Village in 1997, planting seven acres of Syrah, Cabernet Sauvignon, and Merlot grapes, with small amounts of Malbec and Petite Verdot. Despite the theories of "wine experts" who believed that the area couldn't produce great grapes for wine, Bill believes that the mesoclimates available on his acreage allow him to structure his estate wines from great fruit. However, they do make it difficult to harvest since the fruit ripens at different rates.

Although the vineyard is his passion and he enjoys making wine, Bill admits that the work never goes away. Although he was seeking retirement, he finds he's working harder than ever. Fortunately, he has a great deal of help from his family, particularly his son-in-law, Frank.

With his first vintage in 2000, Bill established his winery as "essentially unlike any other winery in the world." He believes that each winery should be distinctively different, preserving unique olfactory memories that help people recall when they tasted a particular wine.

Parson's goal is to produce "big, serious, age-worthy wines." That goal starts in the vineyard where he lets his fruit ripen past what many in the Carmel Valley view as prime picking time. The resulting wine is high in alcohol, but elegant in structure, allowing it to be paired with foods that can equal it in complexity, as well as being an enjoyable beverage by itself. "I'm right to make the wine I want to make," Bill says.

Bill Parsons

The first Parsonage vintages have been well-respected by the wine community. These wines are for the serious collector, and the winery isn't open to the casual weekend taster. However, for those who wish to add a case or two of world-class wine to their cellar, a call to the winery can secure an appointment.

Bill's wife, Mary Ellen, creates quilts in her small art studio on the property. Some of these serve as models for Parsonage wine labels. As she designs and stitches, Bill works hard to continue to meet the reputation he's established for his wines in a few short years.

River Ranch Vineyard

Bill Stahl fell in love with wine in 1968 while attending the University of Southern California. That's when this Monterey County native started collecting wine. He was quite delighted when his sister built a weekend home in Carmel Valley in the late 1970s. "Gee, you need some landscaping," he said.

It was 1983 before Bill planted the two-acre vineyard. Since he was a great Burgundy fan, he decided to try his hand with Chardonnay and Pinot noir varietal grapes. With the cool afternoon breezes at the lower end of the Carmel Valley, he felt that the location could bring out the Burgundy flavors he was seeking.

Bill Stahl

Bill confesses that the vineyard is a constant battle with every type of critter, especially gophers. He nets the vineyard every year; otherwise he loses half the grapes to the birds. Although it is not strictly organic, Bill notes that not much goes on the vineyard that isn't natural. Once the vines were established, he didn't water them anymore.

His first vintage in 1987 didn't have the quality he wanted in his wine, and he has worked hard in the intervening time to get it right. He picks his grapes based on acid, pH and sugar in the fruit, harvesting in the early hours of the morning, carefully sorting the grapes before crushing, and eliminating under-ripe or overripe fruit.

The decision-making process of winemaking intrigues Bill. Every year is different in terms of the quality of grapes produced, variations in barrels and a myriad of different details that make the job a challenge. Bill has spent a number of years reading about, collecting and drinking wine to determine the direction he wants to take his wine.

The Chardonnay is fermented in stainless steel prior to barreling. Both the Pinot noir and the Chardonnay are barreled in French oak barrels — a year for the Chardonnay and a year and a half for the Pinot noir.

With these techniques, Bill is able to produce a wine that is a complement to food, which he believes is the best way to have it. River Ranch wines have a reasonable complexity so that eating and drinking will both be enhanced. He enjoys the thrill every year of trying to produce a better wine.

Bill notes with a smile that there are no financial highpoints with the size of his operation. However, he likes seeing someone enjoying his wine at another table when he's out at a restaurant, knowing that others are sampling his creation.

River Ranch Vineyard

P.O. Box 167
Monterey, CA 93940
Annual Production: 350 cases estate wine; 800 cases total
Wine made with cooperation of Robert Talbott Vineyard in Gonzales
Winery Owners: Bill and Laura Stahl

Access
Not open for tastings

Wines
Chardonnay, Pinot noir

San Saba Vineyards

San Saba Vineyards

820 Park Row #629
Salinas, CA 93901
Phone: 831-753-7222; 800-998-7222
Fax: 831-753-7227
email: sansaba@sansaba.com
Web site: www.sansaba.com
Annual Production: 8,000 cases
Labels: San Saba Vineyard, Bocage
Winemaker: Jeff Ritchey
Winery Owners: Mark and Barbara Lemmon

Access
Tasting Room:
19 E. Carmel Valley Rd.
Carmel Valley, CA
Phone: 831-659-7322
(Second tasting room to open in the future)
Open daily 11–4 Sat.–Sun. in winter; 11–5 Thurs.–Sun. in summer

Tastings
Tasting fee: $3.50, refundable with purchase
Wines: Chardonnay, Sauvignon blanc, Cabernet Sauvignon, Merlot, Pinot noir

Sale of wine-related items? Yes

Lion's Pride Wine Club
Shipment of two wines quarterly at about $35 plus shipping per shipment

Picnics and Programs
Participates in Monterey County Vintners and Growers Association events

The lions on the label of San Saba wine are a perfect symbol for the care and pride that Mark Lemmon brings to the winery and vineyard he's owned in Monterey County for close to 30 years.

Mark grew up in Texas where wine was part of his family life. Then, however, the wine served was French since Mark's father was a Francophile, a common bias before California wines improved in quality. In 1972 Mark began investing in Monterey County vineyard property. Deciding that he wanted to have a more intimate relationship with his own vineyard, Mark purchased land at the intersection of Foothill and Ft. Romney Roads near River Road in the mid-1970s. Mark's vision of a River Road wine corridor is now beginning to blossom.

Looking back over 30 years, Mark Lemmon knows that setting his vineyard and winery in Monterey County was the right decision. In the mid-1970s U.C. Davis was touting Monterey County as the last great place to raise grapes. The U.C. Davis professors weren't completely accurate about what varietal vines to plant or where to plant them in the early days of the county's grape boom, however. Mark went through the same angst as his neighbors did watching the problems of non-ripening Cabernet Sauvignon in parts of the county. Mark grafted his Cabernet Sauvignon vines over to Sauvignon blanc and planted new sections of vineyard with Pinot noir vines — a much better match for the climate and *terroir*.

In Mark Lemmon's opinion, Monterey County is a unique and wonderful place to farm. Although it's less frenetic than Napa and Sonoma, Mark believes there is an energy and closeness to the land shared by the Monterey County growers and winemakers that is hard to find in other wine regions. Monterey County emphasizes good farming methods, a factor that most winemakers agree is crucial to good wine production. Mark also notes that his Monterey neighbors are incredibly cooperative and supportive — lending equipment and room to stay when needed.

Starting his vineyard took a great deal of time and money. Mark especially remembers the deer challenge and the fencing that was required to solve the problem. He farms his land in a sustainable method, replacing minerals in the soil to improve it when needed. He doesn't believe in extreme methods, but maintains a focus on ways of keeping the soil healthy. "I don't want the land to get scurvy," he quips. "I believe in preventive medicine."

Mark Lemmon

Mark is in the Dallas, Texas office of San Saba Vineyards on a daily basis, performing long distance hands-on management of the vineyard and winery construction, and working closely with his winemaker and vineyard manager. He frequently flies from Dallas to Monterey County to get a closer look at exactly what is going on with the land, vines and buildings.

From the beginning, Mark has dreamt of building a winery and tasting room on his vineyard property. (The current tasting room is in Carmel Valley.) He's been in what is termed an "alternate bond position" since the beginning of San Saba. This means he is allowed to use his bond at another winery. It also means he's never quite first in line; consequently standard controls are more difficult, and standards are important to Mark.

The dream came true in 2004 when ground was broken for a winery/tasting room on the vineyard property. (San Saba will also keep the tasting room in Carmel Valley.) The new facility will allow Mark to grow the business to approximately 20,000 cases of wine a year, an amount he believes will retain the current high-quality, hand-crafted style.

The name San Saba comes from a mission close to the Lemmons' home in Texas. It's fitting because the vineyard is less than a mile from the Soledad Mission. Mark searched high and low through the art community to find the appropriate picture for the San Saba label. He finally found it on his own dining room wall. The painting, of a pride of African lions in the Kalahari Desert of Botswana, was created by Rosa Bonheur, a nineteenth-century animal painter. The label designers felt that it would attract male customers in restaurants (traditional wine purchasers), but Mark confesses that they've found "the ladies like it a lot."

The lady in Mark's life is his wife, Barbara, his devoted companion and sounding board. According to Mark she has great judgment and a wonderful palate — two of the most valuable tools in a winery business!

After 35 wonderful and successful years as a doctor in Dallas, Mark retired and sold his practice to a young doctor. He'll probably stay in Texas, leaving the day to day management of his vineyard to Steve McIntyre, an experienced

San Saba vineyard and new winery/tasting room (under construction)

Monterey County vineyard manager,[1] and the winery to Jeff Ritchey, a winery consultant with experience in many wineries, including Clos La Chance in the Santa Cruz Mountains.[2] However, Mark will provide the leadership to insure that the winery will serve his wine consumers as well as he served his patients during his 35 years as a doctor. He believes that if you provide fine wine at an honest value, people will come back again and again to try the wine.

Mark and Barbara Lemmon have a lion's pride in the wine they make.

---

[1] See McIntyre Vineyards, page 104.
[2] See *Mountain Vines, Mountain Wines* for more information on Clos La Chance.

51

Talbott Vineyards

Talbott Vineyards

Web site:
www.talbottvineyards.com
Annual Production: about 30,000 cases
Labels: Talbott, Case, Logan, Kali-Hart
Winemaker: I.C. (Sam) Balderas
Winery Owners: Robert and Cynthia Talbott

Access
Tasting Room:
53 West Carmel Valley Rd.
Carmel Valley, CA 93924
Phone: 831-659-3500
Fax: 831-659-3515
email: tastingroom
@talbottvineyards.com
Open 11–5 Wed.–Mon.

Tastings
Tasting fee: $6
Wines: Chardonnay, Pinot noir, Syrah

Sales of wine-related items? Yes

Talbott Vineyards Wine Club
Various levels available; shipments of two to twelve bottles every three months costing from $65–$350 each; discounts available

Picnics and Programs
Participates in Monterey County Vintners and Growers Association and Carmel Valley Winegrowers Association events

Robert (Robb) Talbott believes that creating wine is the most exciting business he could ever pursue; it's never boring. He is able to design, do construction, drive tractors, create a great product and more. Robb does this all with the spirit and energy of a child discovering a new toy.

Yet underneath this *joi de vivre,* is the dedication to excellence he learned as a child crawling around under his parents' tie-creating table. As Robert Sr. and Audrey developed their clothing business, they taught their son the value of maintaining excellence. They showed him that decisions should be based on quality, not the dollar, and that he must possess the fortitude to make the hard decisions. Through the years Robb has leaned on these values to create his well-respected wine.

However, the gods conspired to test Robb's mettle through his early years of winemaking. Between 1982 and 1990, he had to drill seven wells in order to get enough water to insure his vines' survival. While the vintage of 1983 was good, the 1984 vintage was not up to Robb's standards. True to his dedication to quality, Robb never released his wine that year; the lesson of quality over economics which he learned from his parents triumphed. During that same period the winery was hit by a truck, and Robb had to replace his entire staff for one reason or another. In 1987, his vineyard was hit by a hard frost. Through all of this Robb persevered. He had worked too hard to see his dream die.

There were many pluses during those years as well, including the birth of his three children: Sarah Case, Robert Logan and Kalin Hart. Each child has a wine named in his or her honor. Sam Balderas, previously a production manager

Photo: Casey Dawes

Robb Talbott

Robb attended Colorado College to major in fine art and pursued that occupation for a few years, until a family emergency brought him back to the west coast to help with the family business, which he continues to run. After he met and married his wife, Cynthia, they moved to a ridge high above Carmel Valley. There, in 1982, they began to plant grapes in what was to become one of the most prized vineyards in Monterey County, the Diamond T Vineyard.

at Mirassou Vineyard, joined the company as winemaker. Sam's winemaking philosophy had been formed by experience working at Martin Ray Winery when it was in the Santa Cruz Mountains.[1] Through this experience, Sam learned the traditional European hands-on approach that agreed with the winemaking ideas of the Talbotts.

In 1983 the Talbotts built a winery on land in the Cachagua Valley area of Carmel Valley, a location several miles southeast of the Diamond T Vineyard. The first six vintages were made in that winery, with Robb involved in the winemaking even after Sam joined his team in 1986. Robb has a passion for everything regarding winemaking, from the expression of its origin in the soil to the label that adorns the bottle. In fact, Robb's labels are inspired by a bottle he dug out of the ground near the ghost town of Crested Butte in Colorado. It was the only wine bottle he ever found with a crest.

However, Robb found winemaking in the Cachagua Valley overwhelmingly difficult. Bringing grape trucks up the winding roads tested the patience of both the drivers and Robb. In addition, he wanted more control over the source of his grapes. When a 110-acre ranch on the Santa Lucia Highlands became available, the Talbotts purchased it.

In contrast to the almost soil-free chalky shale of the Diamond T, the new property had incredibly rocky, sandy loam soil with superb drainage. Both vineyards are exposed to the cooling effects of the Monterey Bay fog, allowing them to have a long, mild growing season. The winery itself was completed in 1990. (Bernardus now owns the old Talbott winery.) In 1994 Robb purchased the Sleepy Hollow Vineyards, 450 acres also located on the Santa Lucia Highlands. Sleepy Hollow Vineyard is composed of gravelly loam soil. This final purchase has insured that Robb retains control over the source of his fruit; all Talbott wines are estate grown, although they only use 15 to 18 percent of the fruit they grow.

Through the last 22 years of winemaking, Robb has enjoyed both his family and the challenges of the wine business. His parents supported the venture from the very beginning, although his father died in 1986, and his mother more recently in 2004. Robb's wife, Cynthia, has been his constant partner, helping in the good times and the bad. It's too early to see if any of the three children will enter into the business that bears their names. The eldest daughter, Sarah, is a pre-school teacher; Robb's son is a firefighter and Emergency Medical Technician (EMT), and the youngest daughter, Kalin, is leaning towards a career in fashion. Robb believes his children need to follow their own passion and inner soul, just as he did. "Love what you are doing," Robb advises. "Have passion to create something and you'll succeed."

---

[1] See *Mountain Vines, Mountain Wines* or *Vineyards in the Sky* for more information on Martin Ray.

Talbott tasting room

Wines of Carmel

Wines of Carmel

P.O. Box 1277
Carmel Valley, CA 93924
Phone: 831-659-0750
Fax: 831-659-0750
email: info@winesofcarmel.com
Web site:
www.winesofcarmel.com
Annual Production: 750 cases
Winemaker: Lynn Sakasegawa
Winery Owners: Paul Stokes and
Lynn Sakasegawa

Access
Open by invitation; private
tastings

Tastings
No tasting fee
Wines: Chardonnay, Cabernet
Sauvignon, Merlot, Pinot noir

Wine Club
Three bottles once a year at $60–
$95 per shipment

Picnics and Programs
Participates in Monterey County
Vintners and Growers Association
and Carmel Valley Winegrowers
Association events

Paul Stokes and Lynn Sakasegawa are perfectly happy taking dramatic actions. In 1989 they quit their jobs and sailed away from reality to ports unknown. They were aboard their sailboat in the Panama Locks when Lynn accepted Paul's proposal of marriage. Reality catches up with even the most dedicated adventurers, however, and it became necessary for Paul and Lynn to work again. They settled in California and stuck to regular jobs until Paul grew restless. One morning in 1997, he woke up and declared that they should plant a vineyard. A short time later, Lynn found herself helping Paul put in six acres of vineyard in Hidden Hills in Carmel Valley.

The vineyard is planted on the southwest exposure of steep mountain slopes. A sense of open nature surrounds the vineyards, as well as the home Paul and Lynn have recently built that looks over their vineyards and small valley. Paul says that walking through the vines is like removing himself from the rush of life, giving him time to listen to the owls, rustling critters and other sounds of nature. While it's an idyllic life, the setting belies all the work the couple put into their vineyards, their wine and their day jobs.

Lynn is a CPA and Paul is a marine engineer. For many of us, their jobs coupled with managing their vineyard would be sufficient. However, they weren't entirely satisfied and decided to expand their home winemaking into a public venture. Their first release was a 2001 Chardonnay.

Lynn is the primary winemaker, having only one complaint about winemaking: "All the things to make wine are big and I'm small! But that's life when you're small."

Paul and Lynn aspire to express the unique *terroir* of their vineyard through their wines. The vineyard experiences warm days and foggy nights; the chalky soil contributes to the mineral flavor underlying the flavor of their wines. Paul calls the effort to create the flavors of a Wines of Carmel wine an "enigma wrapped in a conundrum."

Both the vineyard and the winery are cared for with as little intervention as possible. As the couple points out, they live on the vineyard, so they keep chemical use on their land to a minimum. The same applies to their winemaking. Their small winery is a state-of-the-art, gravity-fed facility. They don't have a forklift and they don't need pumps. Everything is done so they "don't beat the wine up," but preserve its natural essence.

Paul Stokes and Lynn Sakasegawa take joy in their lives as vineyard owners and winemakers, and express it in everything they do that is connected with their winery. They regard it as a "lifetime experiment" that will keep Paul from getting too restless in the near future.

Paul Stokes and Lynn Sakasegawa

River Road . . . cliffs appearing on the right . . . the valley laid out below . . . seasons change . . . squares of green become brown and then another shade of green again . . . lime green . . . forest green . . . blue green . . . vineyard green . . . a prickly pear cactus farm . . . a mission off in the distance . . . Foothill . . . wine corridor . . . a seismic fault dividing the bench land from the valley . . . sitting on a tasting room deck . . . view across the valley to the Gabilan Mountains

Burnstein-Remark Winery

Burnstein-Remark Winery's entry into the Los Angeles Wine Competition in 2003 was, to the casual observer, a pretentious offering by a young winery. However, a casual observer wouldn't know the depth of experience that lay behind the unassuming, hand-labeled bottle. Still, several months after the entry into the competition, Joel Burnstein was home with a brief illness, when he received an interesting phone call.

"Where can I buy some Marilyn Remark wine?" the caller asked.

"Who's calling and how do you know we make it?" Joel replied.

"Haven't you heard?"

"Heard what?"

"I just stopped by the L.A. show and you won the whole thing!"

Joel and Marilyn Remark, his long time partner, were amazed. They hadn't counted much on their entry, unsure if wine awards really meant anything. They have since found out that they do. The Grenache that won the L.A. award has received over 90 points in *Wine Enthusiast* and *Wine Spectator* magazines. Their Syrah and Marsanne are poised to follow.

Joel Burnstein and Marilyn Remark

So how did Marilyn Remark wines become an "overnight success"?

As is true with most overnight successes, years of effort went into the launch of the winery. In 1989, fed up with being "rich and poor, rich and poor — all in the same day," Joel Burnstein quit his job as a floor trader with the Pacific Coast Stock Exchange and started taking enology classes at Fresno State University. He spent his senior year as an intern at Sterling Vineyards in Napa Valley where he was in charge of experimental wines. In that position, Joel determined the effects of different variables (such as different yeasts with the same varietal wine) to provide the enologist or winemaker with information needed to make decisions about their wines. This position gave Joel a great deal of experiential knowledge in a short amount of time. It also helped him refine what he did and didn't like about the essence of different styles and varieties of wine.

Joel then moved to Jekel in 1991 and to San Saba in 1995, staying at the San Saba Winery until he was ready to move out on his own in 2004.

Joel and Marilyn base their winemaking process on what they have learned on their trips to France, as well as Joel's years in the wine business. Joel believes that winemaking is a simple process: "You get the best grapes you can get and don't screw it up."

Because the winery is small, Joel is able to get fruit from outstanding vineyards (that he is unable to name); fruit he couldn't get if he was running a larger operation. During harvest he focuses on the physiological ripeness of the grapes in order to pick the best fruit for his wine. Once they are crushed, he nurses the wine to obtain the particular flavors that he has in mind, with as little interference as possible.

Joel is passionate about his winemaking and believes that wine is an important part of life. He says that no matter how full your life is, there's always room for a good bottle of wine.

Burnstein-Remark Winery

645 River Rd.
Salinas, CA 93908
Phone: (831) 455-9310
Fax: (831) 455-9291
email: joel@remarkwines.com
Web site: www.remarkwines.com
Annual Production: about 2000 cases
Winemaker: Joel Burnstein
Winery Owners: Joel Burnstein and Marilyn Remark

Access
Open by appointment
(Tasting room opening shortly after this book goes to print; call winery for more information)

Tastings
No tasting fee
Wines: Roussanne, Grenache, Marsanne, Petite Syrah, Syrah, Rosé, Rhône-style blend

Hahn Estates/
Smith & Hook

Nicky Hahn wanted to create a business for his children, giving them a good start owning an endeavor that could be passed on to future generations. He loved land and felt that a winery offered a diversity of duties, while providing a greater return on investment than the average American farm. A Swiss citizen, Nicky looked at several countries before deciding to purchase land for his winery in America. (Hahn also owns a 46,000-acre nature preserve in Africa and polo grounds in Australia.)

"Every business is a challenge," Hahn says. The idea, he says, is to get your product into the consumer's hands and his money into your pockets, and have him very happy with the transaction.

Adam LaZarre, head winemaker at Hahn Estates/Smith & Hook since 2001, is passionate about the continual learning process of making wine. "If I made the perfect wine," he says, "I'd have to quit." Raised in the Finger Lakes region of New York, Adam grew up around wine. During a stint in the Navy, he spent time in Puget Sound. There he began to go to a neighborhood wine shop, Grape Expectations. The owner,

Adam LaZarre

Nicky purchased the Smith and Hook ranches and four other vineyards (about 1,400 acres) in 1974. He believed that great Cabernet Sauvignon could be grown on the highlands of the Santa Lucia Mountains, and awards for Smith & Hook wines have proven his vision correct. Nicky began the Hahn brand (Hahn means rooster in German) in 1991 to provide a distinct style for other varietal wines, leaving the Smith & Hook name for Cabernet Sauvignon. More recently, the Rex Goliath brand was created for wines at a lower price point.

Mary Pierce, taught Adam about different types of wines. Adam credits Mary with nurturing his budding enthusiasm for wine and returned 15 years after leaving Puget Sound to tell her that she was responsible for his becoming a winemaker.

Once his career path was determined, Adam chose to go to Fresno State University. He believes that his education was more practical than what he would have received at the research-oriented U.C. Davis. During

Hahn Estates/ Smith & Hook Vineyard overlooking the Salinas Valley

one of his first classes, he recalls, he and his fellow students were given five tons of French Columbard grapes and told to make wine. If they had any questions, they could ask. The courses covered all types of winemaking issues — from actually making wine to fixing a forklift.

After stints as an assistant winemaker at Jekel and Riverland Vineyards (part of Blackstone), Adam moved to Hahn Estates/Smith & Hook. Although Adam's style leans towards "big, lush, explosive wines," he believes that everyone in the winemaking team has opinions that are important to the end result. "The best creations are born out of disagreements," he says.

Adam lives and breathes the winery business; he is passionate about his own, as well as others' wine. "I create something that people enjoy and that gives me such a rush," he says, while admitting that it does have a tendency to take over his life.

Like many other winemakers, Adam believes that the work of winemaking is done in the vineyard. In the case of Hahn Estates/Smith & Hook, these vineyards include 1,000 acres spread over seven vineyards: four on the Santa Lucia Highlands, one in Arroyo Seco and two in Paso Robles. The vines are cropped to produce

two tons an acre. Adam spends a lot of time in the vineyards during harvest, determining when to pick based on the "physiological grapeness" of the fruit. He tends to pick when the grapes are high in sugar and adjusts for it in the winery. Although there is a large volume, Adam tends his wine as if he was in a small winery, hand punching some reds during primary fermentation. Some wines are blended prior to being aged almost entirely in French oak barrels. Adam believes in blending different lots of the same varietal wine to add a variety of spices.

A trip to the winery tasting room provides a chance to sample the different wines, but also to envelop yourself in a stunning view that covers most of the Salinas Valley. On a clear day you can see the Pinnacles National Monument and catch a glimpse of Chalone vineyards. As you wander through the tasting room with its varied collection of food-and-wine related offerings, you can decide which wine to have with your lunch. Then you can retire to the picnic tables, enjoying the view and the fruit of the winegrowers' labors.

Morgan Winery

Morgan Winery

590 Brunken Ave., Suite C
Salinas, CA 93901
Phone: 831-751-7777
Fax: 831-751-7780
Web site: www.morganwinery.com
Annual Production: 38,000 cases
Labels: Morgan, Crow's Roost
Winemaker: David Coventry
Winery Owners: Dan and Donna
Lee

Access
Not open for tastings

Wines
Chardonnay, Sauvignon blanc,
Pinot noir, Syrah, Côtes du Crow's
(blend)

Picnics and Programs
Participates in Monterey County
Vintners and Growers Association
events

In 1996, Dan Lee, owner of Morgan Winery, was able to bring his dream of owning his own vineyard to fruition. Because he believes that wine is primarily made in the vineyard, he purchased 65 acres of choice vineyard property in the Santa Lucia Highlands, and spent the next several years developing the soil and planning and planting the 45-acre vineyard. He named the Double L Vineyard, short for double luck, after his twin daughters, Annie and Jackie.

Because the soil of his new property was poor in nutrients, Dan determined that he would farm organically, rebuilding the soil through the use of compost and irrigating with the cleanest water he could find within the property. Once satisfied with the soil's richness, he spent the next three years planting 12 different clones of Pinot noir, six clones of Chardonnay and two clones of Syrah that he had developed from bench grafts. He's also one of the first to use the new Dijon clones for Pinot noir.

Dan finds the notion of yield per acre somewhat misleading, since it's dependent on the number of plants per acre. Within his vineyard, he produces about six pounds of fruit per vine, with about 1,500 plants per acre. The organic nature of his vineyards excites Dan because it yields more minerality, color and structure to the wine, particularly the red varietal wines.

Dan Lee grew up in Turlock, California, the son of an office supply store owner. When he started at U.C. Davis in the early 1970s, he studied veterinary medicine. He notes that the early 1970s were a time of change. People were going "back to the land" and entering non-glamorous professions — working more for the satisfaction of their souls than the size of their bank accounts. In this atmosphere Dan found that viticulture and winemaking appealed to him with the blend of agriculture, science and art, and he switched his major.

While pursuing his master's degree in enology, Dan worked at different wineries to obtain hands-on training. He began full-time winemaking at Jekel in 1978. He reminisces that he spent most of his time eating, sleeping and working as he got the Jekel winery up and running. In the initial phase of the winery, Dan was content with both the operation and the quality of the wine. When Jekel's target changed to creating a larger case volume using inexpensive fruit, Dan felt a need for change. In 1983, Dan left Jekel by mutual agreement and began to work part-time for Durney Winery (now Heller). By 1985 he was able to devote himself full-time to his own winery.

Dan believes that if you do it right in the vineyard, it makes what you do in the winery an easier task. His wines are well-received and in 2003, he was named San Francisco Chronicle's "Winemaker of the Year."

Eventually, Dan Lee plans to move the winery from its present location in Salinas to his vineyard in the Santa Lucia Highlands. He'll add a tasting room there as well. While you are waiting for the tasting room to be built, however, be sure to search out these award-winning wines in the stores, restaurants and multiple-winery tasting rooms in Monterey County.

Dan Lee

Paraiso Vineyards

Paraiso Vineyards

38060 Paraiso Springs Rd.
Soledad, CA 93960
Phone: 831-678-0300
Fax: 831-678-2584
email:
info@paraisovineyards.com
Web site:
www.paraisovineyards.com
Annual Production: about 15,000 cases
Winemaker: David Fleming
Winery Owners: Smith Family

Access
Open 12–4 Mon.–Fri.; 11–5 Sat.–Sun.

Tastings
No tasting fee
Wines: Chardonnay, Riesling, Pinot noir, Syrah

Sale of wine-related items? Yes

Angel's Share Club
Shipments of three bottles every four months costing about $50 each

Picnics and Programs
Picnic facilities; private and public events; participates in Monterey County Vintners and Growers Association events

Living in the country and growing grapes, according to Rich Smith, founder of Paraiso Vineyards, is a pleasure that is full of challenges. "Fifty percent of the business plan belongs to Mother Nature," he adds, "and she never comes to meetings." It's Mother Nature's contribution (or lack of contribution) to the winery business that reminds a successful farmer to be humble.

The seeds of a farmer's life were sown in Rich's youth. He grew up on a 4H farm in Contra Costa County and in 1968 received his degree in agricultural science and management from U.C. Davis. After his return from Vietnam, Rich used that degree to work in a lab performing soil, water and plant analysis. In 1973 he and his wife, Claudia, moved to the Salinas Valley and began planting vines on the 400 acres of land that would become Paraiso Vineyards. Today, Rich and his son, Jason, manage approximately 3,000 acres of vineyards throughout Monterey, using the grapes not only for their own wines, but providing fruit to such wine notables as Hess, Beringer, Mondavi and many others.

Like many growers in the area, Rich Smith believes that Monterey County is a unique agricultural area. The Salinas Valley shows a great deal of climate variation from its northern regions, which receive more of the Monterey Bay fog, to the hotter, drier climate of the Hames Valley. By two in the afternoon, the Paraiso vineyard is already cool and by five p.m. it can be quite cold. Even within the vineyard there is a wide range of total heat units, due to variations in wind, sun and soil. The benefit to this is that many different varietal grapes can be planted in relative proximity. Despite the great range of microclimates, varieties and clones of grapes, Rich has managed to harvest on close to the same day each year for individual vineyard blocks because the climate from season to season is consistent.

Sustainable agriculture requires effort every day, Rich believes, both in his vineyards and throughout the county. He works closely with the Central Coast Vineyard Team which systematically asks questions about irrigation, pest control and viticulture routines in order to insure richer soil, undiminished water resources, and air quality throughout the county. Rich believes that it is the responsibility of every business owner, inside and outside the wine industry, to improve the environment.

Wine production under the original Paraiso Springs name was begun in 1988; Phillip Zorn was winemaker from 1989 to 1997. The position has now been filled by Rich's son-in-law, David Fleming. Paraiso Vineyards has recently embarked on a new plan to enlarge and improve the winemaking operations, including building

Rich Smith

a new winery on the property, scheduled for completion in 2005. Their aim is to create a mid-sized brand (25,000 to 30,000 cases a year) in order to sustain the business effectively.

David's aim in the winery is to complement his family's efforts in the vineyard. According to Rich, the wines need to reflect "this property and this family," and stand apart from everyone else. The Cabernet Sauvignon and Pinot noir wines are based on the Burgundian style with an emphasis on balance. These wines shouldn't be over-extracted, but show substantial flavor, color and texture. The Smiths believe that there are two commercial styles of Syrah — the Rhône style and that of the Australian Shiraz. Paraiso's Syrah has a foot in each camp, Rich believes, having the finesse of the Rhône, but with a little more horse power. The family must be doing something right as Paraiso's two Syrah offerings finished in the top five of their category in the annual compilation of *California Wine Winners*. Overall, Paraiso finished first nationally with the most medals per entry in the nine major professional judgings of that compilation.

The tasting room is bright and cheery with a great view of the Salinas Valley. In addition to the great wines and view, the room is full of eclectic merchandise purchased by Claudia and her daughter-in-law, Jennifer, on their frequent buying trips. The annual air show is a premier event sponsored by the winery. The Fountain Terrace, next to the tasting room, is open for private and corporate events.

Paraiso is a family business; nepotism reigns high according to Rich. Everyone is involved to some degree or another, although Claudia is devoting herself to being a full-time grandmother these days. The family enjoys all aspects of the wine business. Along with Jason Smith as vineyard manager and David Fleming as winemaker, Jason's wife, Jennifer Murphy-Smith, runs the tasting room. David's wife, Kacy, also works in sales. The two young families have three children each, insuring the supply of young winemakers for the future of their aptly named vineyard and winery. Paraiso means paradise.

Winter pruning at Paraiso Vineyards

Pavona Wines

Pavona Wines

Phone: 831-646-1506
Fax: 831-649-8919
email: info@pavonawines.com
Web site: www.pavonawines.com
Annual Production: about 5,000 cases
Winemaker: Aaron Mosely
Winery Owner: Richard Kanakaris

Access
Time pending relocation; call or check web site

Tastings
No tasting fee
Wines: Chardonnay blanc, Petite Syrah, Pinot noir, Syrah, Zinfandel

Sale of wine-related items?   Yes

Club Pavona
Two bottles, four to six times a year for $49 (including shipping, taxes, etc.); events for club members.

Picnics and Programs
Participates in Monterey County Vintners and Growers Association events

As a self-described "huge Paul McCartney fan," Richard Kanakaris couldn't be happier. Pavona wines were selected by McCartney for the Garland Appeal Wine Project, an organization dedicated to supporting breast cancer research and the healing power of music. Richard is very excited. But then again, Richard is excited about anything and everything having to do with life.

Kanakaris has been involved in the wine business for a long time, serving in a wine bar at the age of 21 and continuing his interest by writing for magazines, working in tasting rooms and eventually moving to public relations and sales. In 1993 he became general manager for Monterey Peninsula Winery. It was there that Richard began to conceive of owning his own winery.

Richard envisioned Pavona Wines (*pavona* means peacock in Italian) as a winery devoted to artisan-style wines with a richer flavor than many California wines. He also wanted to promote the use of Monterey County fruit. He refined his vision by determining that he wouldn't go head to head with other wineries producing Chardonnay, Cabernet Sauvignon or Merlot.

Pinot blanc was the first wine he created, but he found it difficult to sell because it was an uncommon varietal wine. After some other experimentation, he's primarily settled on Syrah, Pinot noir and Zinfandel — wines that Richard claims have the three fastest growing varietal wine sales in the United States. Pavona Wines also produces a Chardonnay blanc that is a blend of Chardonnay and Pinot blanc. It is this wine that will be used in the Garland Appeal Wine Project.

Currently, Richard obtains 80 percent of his fruit from the Monterey County area, predominantly in the Santa Lucia Highlands AVA. His Zinfandel grapes come from old vines in Lodi; some other varietal groups are obtained there as well. His aim is to increase the percentage over time. He believes that Monterey County will continue to expand in the number of vineyards planted. The variety of climates within the county supports many different varietal vines if they are planted in the right area. Although he is dedicated to using Monterey grapes, Richard isn't interested in adding vineyards to his own enterprise, believing the agriculture would dilute both his winemaking focus and his capital.

Richard describes Pavona's winemaking style as hand-crafted with minimalist intervention. He is helped in this vision by Aaron Mosely, an award-winning winemaker with an impressive background. In addition to numerous degrees, Mosely has worked with many well-recognized winemakers, such as André Tchelistcheff and Mike Grgich.

Richard Kanakaris

Pavona tasting room

Pavona wines are made with fully ripe fruit and little concern for high alcohol levels or tannin. The wines are totally barrel-fermented in combinations of French and American oak barrels. Because he is committed to introducing wine at a variety of prices, Richard has experimented with using oak staves in barrels to reintroduce the wood element without having to purchase costly new barrels. The technique must work well because Pavona wines compete well in blind tastings with pricier wines.

In addition to producing fine wines, Richard believes in marketing. "Just making good wine doesn't sell the wine," he says. This is especially true in the overcrowded wine market of the early 21st century. When he discusses his innovations and "firsts" in the industry, he comes alive, a wound spring of enthusiastic ideas. Pavona wines are focused on a younger demographic than traditional wines and this aim shows clearly in the label, the first holographic label approved by the government. The label goes beyond glittering marketing, however. Pavona Wines were the first to use a bilingual label, targeting Pavona to the growing Hispanic market.

Richard's marketing flair is demonstrated by the shape of his bottles, and his flaunting of industry bottling traditions. For example, his Zinfandel is in a bottle that most vintners use for Pinot noir. His care isn't limited to the bottle. He's never used foils on Pavona wines because of environmental concerns. Instead he uses a B-cap closure (a circle of wax on top of the cork to protect the cork from outside damage) covered with a Pavona emblem.

Recently, Richard was able to open a tasting room in facilities that he shares with Pessagno Winery on River Road near Gonzales. River Road snakes by the cliff that marks the Santa Lucia Highlands, showcasing the Salinas Valley floor and Gabilan Mountains to the east.

Tucked into the barrel room, the tasting room is small and casual. True to Richard's philosophy of introducing good wines at reasonable prices, there's always a sale going on in the tasting room. When he is present, the tasting room vibrates with his excitement and energy. Even when he isn't there, his energy remains in the flashy peacock on his label.

Note: As we went to press, Pavona Wines was in the process of relocating to Marina, CA. Call or visit their website for the latest information.

Pessagno Winery

Pessagno Winery

1645 River Road
Salinas, California 93908
Phone: 831-484-1154
Fax: 831-484-1153
Web site:
www.pessagnowines.com
Annual Production: about 3,000
cases
Winemaker: Stephen L.
Pessagno
Winery Managing Partners:
Stephen L. Pessagno, Don
Barnett, Emanuel Lazopoulos

Access
Open 11–4 Fri..–Sun.
(Hours may be changing; call
ahead)

Tastings
No tasting fee
Wines: Chardonnay, Pinot noir,
Zinfandel, port

Sale of wine related items? Yes

Picnics and Programs
Participates in Monterey County
Vintners and Growers Association
events

After Steve Pessagno helped make his first wine at the age of 16 on his grandfather's ranch in San Jose, he was permanently hooked. For a number of years after that event Steve regarded winemaking only as a "hobby." He graduated with a degree in mechanical engineering in 1980 — a financially safer occupation than winemaking. While Steve was a senior engineer for the Alternative Energy Division of Acurex Corporation, the hobby continued to have a life of its own. By 1982 the home winery outgrew his garage.

It was in 1982 that Steve took a first step towards his current career by working the crush at Kirigin Cellars, a small winery near Gilroy. With that event, the grape's seduction of Steve was complete, and he gave up a "perfectly good career" as an engineer to answer the siren's song.

In February of 1983 Steve became assistant winemaker at Kirigin Cellars, bringing his engineering knowledge with him. Winemaking is frequently a balance between scientific know-how and an instinctive understanding of the fermentation process. At Kirigin, Steve began to understand just how useful his knowledge of combustion heat transfer and fluid dynamics might be in the winery. However, like many other winemakers with engineering backgrounds, Steve was also able to turn off the engineering portion of his brain to embrace the heart of the grape.

Steve earned his wine degree over the next three years, spending much, but not all, of his time at California State University in Fresno, a school he describes as the home of winemakers in "black rubber boots dragging hoses." He received his enology degree from Fresno in 1986.

From 1986 to 1991, Steve worked at Jekel Vineyards, before leaving to work at the newly formed Lockwood Vineyards. While there, he was responsible for upgrading and modernizing the winery to provide an expanded capacity and improve wine quality. He also purchased one of the first cross-flow filters in Monterey County. Relatively new technology, this filter allows finer wine filtration with less abuse of the wine and impact on the environment.

While working at these larger facilities, however, Steve was still haunted by the memory of the small batches of wine he had made as a teenager with his grandfather. So, in 1999 Steve created Pessagno Winery with his friends, Don Barnett and Emanuel Lazopoulos. His goals for the business were simple: obtain the finest fruit and make the finest wine. Steve leverages his

Steve Pessagno

Courtesy Pessagno Winery

knowledge of premium vineyards in Monterey County (Sleepy Hollow, Garys' Vineyard, and Central Avenue Vineyard) to gain access to great fruit. All the varietal grapes are processed in small lots, with various techniques used to achieve a strong mouth feel in his wines.

Even when creating wines from the same varietal grape, Steve's processes vary to take into account the essence of fruit obtained from different locations. For example, for Pinot noir grapes from Garys' Vineyard on the Santa Lucia Highlands, Steve slightly crushes the fruit into small tanks and allows it to cold soak for several days to slowly release flavor and aroma components from contact with the grape skins prior to fermentation. He uses a special type of yeast to slow fermentation and help integrate tannins. The wine is then pressed directly into 100% new French barrels to age for twelve months.

Steve's initial releases achieved a high level of recognition from many wine writers.

In 2004 Steve realized yet another dream, working on arrangements to purchase the Cloninger Winery on River Road. He feels that the Pessagno brand is mature enough to support a facility of his own and the location is perfect — in the middle of great vineyards and wineries such as Morgan, Talbott and Estancia.

Once again, Steve will be faced with revamping a winery to improve capacity. He needs to create a larger capacity than that facility has ever seen, producing close to 20,000 cases of his own wine and also providing custom winemaking for other small-production artisan wineries. Steve is totally swamped with work in the realization of his dream, but reminds himself to stop and "enjoy the process of getting there, rather than just getting there."

The tasting room at the winery will be open Friday through Sunday initially, although Steve believes that it will be expanded to seven days a week at a later point in time.

Steve finds that there's something new to do every day. He makes it a family affair, with his four sons helping him continue a legacy that he received from his grandfather, Anthony Escover, over thirty years ago.

Windmill at Pessagno Winery

Pisoni Vineyards and Winery

P.O. Box 908
Gonzales, CA 93926
Phone: 800-270-2525
Fax: 831-675-2557
email: info@pisonivineyards.com
Web site:
www.pisonivineyards.com
Annual Production: 2,000 cases
Labels: Pisoni, Lucia
Winemaker: Jeff Pisoni
Winery Owners: Pisoni family

Access
Not open for tastings

Wines
Pinot noir, Syrah

Pisoni Vineyards and Winery

Gary Pisoni has bitten a huge chunk of the apple of life and is enjoying every minute of the sensation. Every word he utters, every action he takes, every philosophy he espouses is enlarged by his eagerness to experience life to the fullest and have you join him in the effort.

Drafted at an early age to help his father, Ed Pisoni, handle the eight to ten steers on his dream cattle ranch in the Santa Lucia Highlands, Gary decided that there was a better way to make a living than trying (and failing) to get recalcitrant cattle into a trailer. His solution? To put something in the land and make it grow. That something was grapes.

His father thought it was a crazy idea, but let him go ahead with it. Gary began to put vineyards wherever he could. He obtained the best vine clones and planted them on their own roots — a move many vineyard managers called insane. (Vines are often cloned to phylloxera-resistant rootstock to prevent the disease from killing off a vineyard.) Gary dismissed their concerns with a wave of his hand. The isolation of his vineyards will protect them, he believes. And besides, he says, "fruit from its own roots tastes better."

Any visitor to the 280-acre ranch (45 acres are planted to vines) is likely to get a wild ride. With Gary at the helm of a 1969 jeep, you'll go careening up and down gulleys and ridges.

Gary's corkscrew hair will fling wildly as he tells story after story, his hoarse voice vying with the engine's roar. Blocks of grapes whiz by, named after former girlfriends and his mother, Jane. If he's in a mood to shock you, he might just drop his clothes and soak in the vineyard bathtub to demonstrate how he watches the grapes grow.

Behind all this hedonistic theater, however, there is a passion for the land, agriculture and family that makes Pisoni grapes among the highest priced in the nation. "It's amazing what happens when you work with nature," Gary says.

The family moved into making wine in the 1990s, with its first vintage in 1998. Gary's son, Jeff, is in charge of the winemaking, and Mark, Gary's other son, helps create the wine, as well as tend the family's row crops on the Salinas Valley floor. The young men grew up with winemaking and decided that they had the best opportunity in the family business making small lots of wine. Gary has gratefully turned over the winemaking, since he believes that he made a lot more vinegar in the process of learning the craft than Jeff ever did.

The Pisoni's winemaking philosophy is definitely hands-off, allowing nature to perform the grape creation. Their task, they believe is to amplify the voice of nature without interfering.

Taste Pisoni wine and you can hear the voice of the earth. If you listen very carefully, you'll also hear the echo of Gary's voice roaring over the engine of the 1969 jeep.

Gary Pisoni

Roar Wines

Gary Franscioni's roots are in the Salinas Valley and his heart is in the land. He represents a third generation of farmers, beginning with his grandfather Silvio who immigrated to California from Switzerland in 1886. The family settled down to be small family farmers, growing row crops such as dry beans, potatoes and sugar beets. Throughout his life, Gary has been dedicated to the family business, earning his degree in agribusiness from California Polytechnic Institute in 1976.

Gary might never have deviated from row crops, had it not been for a small side trip he took to Napa in his college years. There he saw the beauty of the vines and was infected by the winegrowing bug. He spent the next 20 years accumulating know-how and cash to begin his own vineyard. Further economic pressures convinced him that it was vital to expand to a new cash crop in order to survive as a small family farmer.

A meticulous grower, Gary set out to create one of the top vineyards in the state. In 1996 he planted Rosella's Vineyard, named after his wife, on 50 acres on the Santa Lucia Highlands that formerly were used for broccoli and romaine lettuce. Today, Rosella's vineyard is comprised of nine acres of Chardonnay vines, 37 acres of Pinot noir and four acres of Syrah.

The physical structure of Rosella's vineyard is the antithesis of what has been called California sprawl, a trellising system that allows limbs of vines to trail to the ground between the rows. Instead Gary has a used a vertical shoot positioning trellis system which keeps the rows compact and clean. With the help of his valued workers, Gary pays a great deal of attention to canopy management. He uses aggressive leaf and stem pulling techniques to shade the fruit when necessary and expose it to the sun to insure correct ripeness. Gary also makes sure that the vines "scream for water."

All of this is intensive farming, but the fruit that comes from Rosella's vineyard, as well as the vineyard Franscioni shares with his boyhood friend, Gary Pisoni, (Garys' Vineyard) is highly prized among winemakers and wine consumers. In 2001, Gary decided to make his own wine to see what other winemakers were doing with his fruit. Besides, he admits, "I like wine."

The Roar wines are made in Santa Rosa by Dianna and Adam Lee who also use Gary's fruit in the Siduri and Novy brands. Gary works closely with them to jointly decide fermentation, blending, barreling and bottling techniques. A relatively new brand, Gary believes Roar will take about ten years to come into its own.

Gary Franscioni remains a farmer at heart, viewing a grape vine as just another plant. However, he adds with a grin, "What's really great is that you can drink it."

Gary Franscioni

Roar Wines

32721 River Road
Soledad, CA 93960
Phone: (831) 675-1681
Fax: (831) 675-1683
email: wine@roarwines.com
Web site: www.roarwines.com
Annual Production: 1,000 cases
Winemakers: Gary Franscioni, Dianna and Adam Lee
Winery Owners: Gary and Rosella Franscioni

Access
Not open for tastings

Wines
Pinot noir, Syrah

Arroyo Seco

Water-carved mountains . . . silt, soil and sand . . . Greenfield potatoes . . . carved cliffs protecting a Sanctuary Vineyard . . . lines of vines fan out into the valley below . . . marked by Arroyo Seco drainage into the Salinas River . . . early vineyards . . . Lohr . . . Meader . . . and more . . .

Carmel Road Winery

Carmel Road Winery, a part of Jackson Family Farms, is a unique entity that is designed to produce wines solely from Monterey County vineyards. One could consider it a small, family winery within the framework of a large one.

Carmel Road Winery began in 1996 with Dan Kleck as the winemaker. He was joined in 1999 by assistant winemaker, Ivan Giotenou, who became winemaker in 2002.

Ivan can trace his family's roots back to the 17th century. His ancestors were farmers in a small village 60 miles southeast of Sofia, Bulgaria. His family had 20 to 30 acres of vineyards and made wine, hauling it to the capital to sell to restaurants. With the advent of communism in the 1940s, everything was nationalized and the family was no longer able to sell wine.

Eventually the family was allowed to return to a quarter of the original property. Ivan's father could make two to three barrels of wine a year from the vines he was able to grow on the land. Ivan has fond memories of the bush vines growing on the south-facing hills of Bulgaria. Although his parents wanted him to study chemistry, Ivan wanted to do what his family had done before communism, and studied winemaking. He left Bulgaria to work the harvest in Australia in 1998.

Ivan worked as an assistant winemaker for a winery in central Victoria, as well as Tuck's Ridge Winery at Mornington Peninsula, also in Victoria. While there, Ivan made wine with Pinot noir grapes for the first time. Pinot noir reminded Ivan of the light-style wine made from the *pamid* varietal grape in his homeland. His destination was always the United States, however, and as soon as he became eligible for his green card, he immigrated to the United States in 1998.

Working for Jackson Family Farms has allowed Ivan to indulge in the winemaking techniques he enjoys. "The more natural the technique, the more beautiful the wine is," he says. With Carmel Road wines, he builds the wine from the vineyard. Ivan believes that the texture of a wine is important, and the process for that begins in the vineyard. Like many winemakers in the area, Ivan has a great appreciation for the varieties of temperature in the Salinas Valley: "The wind is a natural air conditioner, cooling down and preserving the grapes' flavor."

To get the greatest flavors into his wine, Ivan determines when to pick based on taste. Like his predecessor, Ivan is gentle with the grapes as he processes them to make wine. He does not want you to lose the flavor of where the grapes are grown when you taste a Carmel Road wine.

Ivan Giotenou

Carmel Road Winery

37300 Doud Road, Drawer D
Soledad, CA 93960
Phone: 800-273-8558
email: info@carmelroad.com
Web site: www.carmelroad.com
Annual Production: 1,900 cases
Winemaker: Ivan Giotenou
Winery Owners: Jackson Family Farms

Access
Not open for tastings

Wines
Chardonnay, Pinot noir

Scheid Vineyards

Scheid Vineyards

305 Hilltown Rd.
Salinas CA 93908
Phone: 831-455-9990
Fax: 831-455-9998
Web site:
www.scheidvineyards.com
Annual Production: 3,000 cases
Winemaker: Steve Storrs
Winery Owners: Scheid family

Access
Open 11–5 daily

Tastings
Tasting Room:
1972 Hobson Ave.
Greenfield, CA 93927
Phone: 831-386-0316
Fax: 831-386-0127
No tasting fee
Wines: Chardonnay,
Gewürztraminer, Sauvignon
blanc, White Riesling, Cabernet
Sauvignon, Merlot, Pinot noir,
Syrah, Red Table Wine (blend)

Sale of wine-related items? Yes

Picnics and Programs
Picnic area available; participates
in Monterey County Vintners and
Growers Association events

The average wine consumer traveling along Route 101 might stop at the Scheid Vineyards tasting room to enjoy the variety of wines, check out wine-related merchandise and bask in the company of the tasting room personnel. However, if they thought they'd experienced all Scheid had to offer, they would be mistaken. Scheid's primary business is the production and sale of grapes to such wine producers as Chalone Wine Group, Georis Winery, Golden State Vintners, Morgan Winery, Blackstone Winery, Hahn Estates/Smith & Hook Winery, and more. The wines available in their tasting room showcase the grapes Scheid grows.

The vineyards, originally under the name of Monterey Farming Corporation, were established in 1972 by Alfred Scheid and E.F. Hutton and Company as an investment tax shelter. This was a common practice in Monterey County in the late 1960s and 1970s. In 1988, Al Scheid bought out E.F. Hutton and Company to become sole owner, changing the name to Scheid Vineyards in 1989. Today most of the business is controlled by two of Al's children: Scott as CEO and Heidi as Senior VP. The company is also the only publicly traded vineyard company on the NASDAQ Stock Exchange.

The Scheids own 13 distinct vineyards ranging from Soledad to the Hames Valley. Each has its own vineyard manager with overall management direction falling to Senior VP and COO (Chief Operating Officer) Kurt Gollnick. Gollnick is in charge of every grapevine in the company. Vineyards are a serious investment, requiring $15,000 to $18,000 per acre for the first three years. When you define your company as grape growing specialists, as Scheid does, you need to pay serious attention to that investment.

According to Scott Scheid, many wineries prefer to farm out a large portion of their grape growing to a specialist such as Scheid. For small wineries, working with a master viticulturalist is critical to their reputation. Large wineries also need reliable sources of grapes, but need them in large quantities distributed over a wide area.

Frequently, winemakers have specific requirements about how they want their grapes grown. When a company such as Scheid wants to deliver the "best premium wine grapes they can according to winery specifications," a challenge arises. The challenge is intensified by the proximity of blocks of vines farmed for different wineries situated close to each other. For example, winery A's grapes might be in a block that is 15 feet away from the grapes of

Scott Scheid

winery B. Many wineries can't afford to send a winemaker to every vineyard producing grapes for them, especially as harvest approaches — the most critical time in the winery process. The Scheids have helped solve this problem with a product called VitiWatch.®

By using web technology and field instrumentation, VitiWatch® allows winemakers to view data on their own blocks of grapes using the Scheid web site. Historical information is kept, so they can analyze trends against current information to aid their decision-making.

they discovered they had too much good wine on their hands, and decided to sell the extra. Their first vintage was in 1989. Steve Storrs, a Santa Cruz winemaker who has been purchasing grapes from the Scheids since 1988, serves as the Scheid's winemaker as well.[1] In spite of the fact that Scheid is one of the largest independent grape growers in California, the winery is a boutique winery. Most of their wine is sold locally to restaurants, through their tasting room, and as an "annual wine dividend" to their shareholders. (This dividend is described in detail on their web site.)

Grape buds at Scheid demonstration vineyard

The technology in the field allows Scheid to collect information on weather data such as wind conditions (a vital force in the Salinas Valley), rainfall, temperature, etc. Vine analysis is also used to determine the amount of moisture in the vine. Soil analysis provides soil nutrition and water content information. There is also lab data on the fruit to give the winemaker an idea of sugar levels (brix), acidity, pH and other measures. As harvest approaches, the data is collected on a more frequent basis and posted in real time to aid the winemaker in harvest decisions. This powerful approach brings a high-tech look to a low-tech industry.

To insure that their vineyards were producing the high quality of grapes that they intended, the Scheids also made test lots of wine. Eventually,

According to Scott Scheid, Monterey is an incredible wine region that you may not be aware of as you whiz by on U.S. Highway 101. The wine region produces excellent grapes across the spectrum. It is definitely worth your while to stop and explore the Scheid Vineyards tasting room and their demonstration vineyard. It will give you a greater appreciation for the science and viticulture behind the wine you taste. It will also help you understand the true nature of Scheid Vineyards.

[1] For more information on Steve Storrs, see *Mountain Vines, Mountain Wines.*

Ventana Vineyards

Ventana Vineyards

2999 Monterey–Salinas Highway
Monterey, CA 93940
Phone: 831-372-7415
Fax: 831-375-0797
email: info@ventanawines.com
Web site: www.ventanawines.com
Annual Production: 30,000 cases
Labels: Ventana Vineyards,
Meador Estate
Winemakers: Doug Meador and
Reggie Hammond
Winery Owners: Doug and LuAnn
Meador

Access
Open 11–4 daily

Tastings
No tasting fee
Wines: Chardonnay,
Gewurztraminer, Pinot blanc,
Riesling, Dry Rosado, Sauvignon
blanc, Cabernet Sauvignon,
Merlot, Syrah, Pinot noir, Due
Amici (blend of Cabernet
Sauvignon and Sangiovese),
Muscat d'Orange (dessert wine)

Sale of wine-related items? Yes

Ventana Family Wine Club
Shipment of three wines four to
five times a year at about $38 per
shipment; red wine only at about
$48 per shipment; special events

Picnics and Programs
Participates in Monterey County
Vintners and Growers Association
events

As you talk about wine in Monterey County, you begin to hear more and more about the wine growing pioneers of the 1960s and 1970s. One name stands out — that of Doug Meador, founder and owner of Ventana Vineyards. Along with being in the forefront of Monterey winemakers, Meador was (and still is) in the forefront of viticultural and winery innovations.

Meador's opinions about viticulture and enology weren't always valued by the establishment, but he continued to do things he felt were right. If the number of awards he has received for his wines is any indication (by 2004, Ventana wines had received 26 consecutive years of gold and silver medals at major wine competitions), Doug Meador's instincts are accurate. After ten years of being ostracized by the U.C. Davis teaching community, his *avant garde* theories have been accepted as correct.

It was in the spring of 1972 when the Washington state native came to Monterey County after serving six and a half years as a jet pilot, including two tours in Vietnam. He came from a family that farmed apple orchards, which gave him a background in permanent crops. However, he admits that what he knew about grapevines was limited to realizing he had to plant them greenside up!

During the 1960s and 1970s, tax laws made it advantageous to create land trusts as tax shelters.[1] Many large vineyards in Monterey were started under these laws. Doug Meador joined a trust that owned 2,500 acres in the county. During his on-the-job training, Doug immediately started to test his hypotheses about the best way to get the job done.

In 1975 the tax laws changed and Meador rescued 365 acres from the original parcel. That was the foundation of Ventana Vineyard and Meador's ever-evolving knowledge, and experimentation with viticulture and enology.

The change of ownership rules was not only good for Meador, but for Monterey County wines in general. According to Meador, initial plantings in the county integrated a great many wrong ideas, especially given the unique characteristics of the climate. People who planted used the warm climate rules that worked in Napa, planted the wrong varietal vines for the area and were absentee landowners. The result was disastrous for the reputation of Monterey County wines.

Doug Meador strode into this set of problems ready to change the public's opinion. He strongly believed that Monterey County had all the potential for a great wine region, if the vineyard managers would only "follow nature's rules and work within them." Although he didn't walk in knowing all the answers, Meador knew that what

Doug Meador

people were doing at the time wasn't working. He was ready to learn the answers that the county's soil and climate could provide. So he began, and continues to this day, to experiment with theories and to find out what actually happens in Monterey County as opposed to what the pundits say should happen.

Doug Meador's first experiment was with a six-acre Gewürztraminer vineyard that he planted in 1978. In 1981 he harvested 7.3 tons of grapes per acre — an incredible statistic in a region that could barely produce three tons per acre. In addition, he was able to pick earlier than his neighbors which is always a good position for a vineyard manager to be in, given the availability of labor and equipment.

To achieve his high production, Meador had to make his first, but not last, break from the "common wisdom" preached by U.C. Davis at that time. This body of knowledge was based on viticultural development, as well as living with the practicalities of machinery created for harvesting grapes. The U.C. Davis recommendations allowed vineyard managers to plant about 518 vines per acre. Using closer vine spacing, yet leaving vine rows wide enough for conventional machinery, Meador was able to plant 1,210 vines per acre. Continually refining the process, Meador plants up to 2,074 vines per acre today, depending on the varietal grape.

In answer to the challenge that high-yield vineyards produce flabby wines, Meador deliberately made high-intensity wines from his Gewürztraminer vineyard in the mid-1980s, although it isn't his preferred style of wine. It put the critics to rest, however, and Doug went back to thinking.

Since that time, Doug Meador has continued to listen to what the land and climate have to tell him, trying out his theories about everything from planting vines on their own root stock to determining the best source of wood for his wine barrels. He continues to follow his own muse, whether or not it coincides with conventional wisdom. And he will continue to provide advice and help to fellow Monterey County winemakers.

Ventana tasting room entrance

The Ventana Vineyard tasting room is next to Tarpy's Roadhouse, an establishment rich in local Monterey lore. As you stroll around the fieldstone tasting room, sipping wines made from "the most award-winning single vineyard property in America," see if you can taste the difference that Doug Meador's unconventional wisdom makes.

---

[1] See the history chapter for more information.

San Bernabe

Newest AVA . . . largest contiguous vineyard in California . . . Delicato near King City . . . acres and acres of vines . . . 20 square miles

Delicato Vineyards

Delicato Vineyards is the sole occupant of the newly formed San Bernabe AVA, although the company only owns about 50 percent of this AVA's 25,000 plus acres. Tim Wong, director of winemaking, describes the 12,600-acre parcel as one of unique and varied microclimates. Approximately 1,700 acres are planted in row crops, with another 4,800 acres in grape vines. The remaining property is utilized for the non-irrigated farming of barley. The variety of soils and climates creates hundreds of small vineyards within this vast expanse. Delicato has planted 21 different varietal vines in one of the largest contiguous vineyards in California. That's a lot for Chief Operating Officer for the San Bernabe vineyard, Claude Hoover, to handle.

Delicato's history goes back over 80 years. Gasparé Indelicato immigrated to America in 1912 and eventually started working in vineyards near Lodi. In the 1920s he planted grapes around his home, selling most of them to home winemakers in Chicago. His wine cellar was opened after the repeal of Prohibition in 1935. The Indelicato family continued the operation after his death in 1962.

In 1974, the Prudential Insurance and Southdown companies established the vineyard that was to become Delicato's Monterey operation. Delicato purchased 110 acres of the vineyard in 1987 and began to construct the winery, purchasing the remaining acreage in 1988.

Tim Wong describes the Delicato operation as having three essential components. The first is to sell the San Bernabe Vineyard grapes or its juice to other wineries. The second element, and possibly the most complex, is to make wine for other wineries. This involves coping with the diverse style expectations of dozens of different winemakers — each with their own individual techniques and demands. While this is challenging, Tim finds seeing the customer's satisfaction during the winemaking process greatly rewarding.

Finally, Delicato also makes its own set of wines from the Monterey vineyard. "The best grapes from the best vineyard rows from the best vineyard blocks" go into the Vine Select brand, a limited release of about 500 cases per year. The Monterey wines are handled by the San Bernabe winemakers, Ignacio Cruz and James Ewart.

The Monterra brands express the Monterey county flavors and are the most common of the Delicato Monterey brands. A third brand of non-varietal specific wines was recently created. To have fun with the name, Delicato went to an art school to explain their concept of blended wines. They asked the students to create a name and image. The result? Encore!

Tim Wong believes that the Delicato Monterey group is a terrific staff that thrives on challenges, and creating good wines that show true varietal grape characteristics. If they are successful, Wong believes, you'll want to come back for more.

Alisha Isis and Tim Wong

Delicato Vineyards

12001 South Hwy 99
Manteca, CA 95336
Phone: 888-599-4637 or 209-824-3501
Fax: 209-824-3510
email: wine@delicato.com
Web site: www.delicato.com
Annual Production: 1.5 million cases
Director of Winemaking: Tim Wong
Winemakers at San Bernabe: Ignacio Cruz and James Ewart
Winery Owners: Indelicato Family

Access
Open 9–5:30 daily

Tastings
No tasting fee
Wines: Chardonnay, Sauvignon blanc, Cabernet Sauvignon, Merlot, Shiraz, White Zinfandel, red, white and rosé blends under the Encore brand

Sale of wine-related items: Yes

Wine Clubs
Three wine clubs available; shipments range from two bottles six times a year costing about $35 to small shipments quarterly costing about $75; events and other discounts

Picnics and Programs
Participates in Monterey County Vintners and Growers Association events

Once there were cattle . . . now there are vines . . .
warmer than the north . . . the fog doesn't always find
these vines . . . but the wind goes everywhere that isn't
sheltered . . . the sun bakes down in the summer . . .
desolation forces strength in people, animals and crops

Lockwood Vineyard

Towards the southern end of Monterey County, the countryside becomes more lonely and desolate than the denser towns of the north. Cows are more common than humans, and large swaths of vineyards catch the eye. One of these vineyards is Lockwood Vineyard, found near the town with the same name. It's interesting to note that the town's original name was Desolation Flats, perhaps a more apt name for this isolated area.

The climate contains a similar ruggedness, buffeted between the cool fogs of Monterey Bay as they travel down the Salinas Valley and the heat rising from the plains to the county's south. The vineyards can experience a diurnal temperature swing of 60 degrees in just a few hours — from 50 degrees in the morning fog to 110 degrees in midday heat. According to former winemaker Steve Pessagno, the land and climate make Lockwood uniquely suited to growing a wide range of varietal grapes with great success. This isn't true of most other grape growing areas.

In 1981, the founding partners of Lockwood — Paul Toeppen, Phil Johnson and Butch Lindley — planted 1,670 acres on a 1,850 acre parcel in what is now the San Lucas AVA. In addition to the stress of the temperature, the vineyard soil is primarily made up of "Lockwood Shaly Loam," a calcareous chalk-rock which causes the vines to work hard to get the nutrients they need.

The group's initial idea was to have a great vineyard and sell the grapes, but by 1989, they decided that they would like to be able to produce fine estate wines from their vineyard. They set up their winery in an old labor camp and began with approximately 350 cases, winning awards almost immediately. In 1991 Steve Pessagno joined the team.[1]

When the winery began its operation, it could process five tons of grapes an hour — not a very rapid rate for a facility that presently produces 250,000 cases of wine a year (80,000 to 100,000 cases for Lockwood; 150,000 cases in a custom crush operation). In order to handle the volume, the partners substantially upgraded the winery in 1998.

In 2004, Larry Gomez became Lockwood's winemaker. Larry comes from a vineyard family. His uncle had a vineyard in Napa that was ultimately sold to the Screaming Eagle brand, dashing Larry's hopes of working for the family vineyard. The incident didn't dissuade Larry from his dream, however. He received his Masters degree in wine chemistry from Fresno in 1990, and worked at Monterey and Paso Robles wineries during the next 13 years, including a stint at Lockwood.

Larry clearly loves the land and soil that produce the great fruit of Lockwood. He talks about the odd combination of marine deposits and Lockwood soil, considering the Santa Lucia Mountains that currently separate the vineyard from the ocean. He has a farmer's passion for the soil and the food it provides. After all, he notes, soil isn't something that just pops out of a bag at K-mart; it takes eons for it to come alive.

According to Larry, wines are alive; winemakers "just walk alongside and watch it." If you have excellent soil and manage your vines well, you can produce exceptional fruit. Tasting Lockwood wines, Larry believes, is like tasting "vibrant fruit in the glass."

---

[1] See Pessagno Winery, page 66, for more information on Steve Pessagno.

Lockwood Vineyard (photo courtsey Lockwood Vineyard)

Hames Valley

A left crook on a map . . . sheltered from the wind tunnel of the Salinas Valley . . . Percherons and grapes . . . a road to the San Padre National Forest . . . soft heat . . . the marine coolness reaches in to temper the sun . . . Bradley . . . no one further south

Hames Valley Vineyards

According to Shelley Denney, her husband Bob can spin dreams like a web. Fortunately, he also has the determination, as well as Shelley's help, to make them come true.

Returning from Vietnam in the late 1960s, Bob decided to take advantage of the GI Bill to attend U.C. Davis to get a degree in agriculture. While there, he met and married Shelley. The two embarked on a partnership, adventure and love affair that have lasted over 32 years.

After Bob left Davis, he worked on the last apricot and nut orchard left standing in San Jose before the bulldozers finished transforming Silicon Valley into a cement and glass garden. Bob's employer had purchased a large ranch in the San Joaquin Valley and she wanted him to run the ranch. So, Bob and his family moved to the San Joaquin valley.

While working on the ranch, Bob had the opportunity to plant his first wine grapes in 1979. Three years later, he began working for a large agricultural firm, managing approximately 10,000 acres of orchards and vineyards. During this time period, he became the founding chair of the Southern San Joaquin Winegrape Growers Association. The Denneys were successful with both their professional lives and their family (they have three daughters), but were also thinking about a place where they could retire in the future.

They found their ideal location on a return trip from a summer seaside cottage in April 1988. There, in the Hames Valley at the southern end of Monterey County, the Denneys discovered an incredible parcel of land with magnificent water resources. Within five months they had made arrangements to buy the 640 acres of land that served as a foundation for their dream. They were delighted to learn that they were only the third family to own the property since it was first homesteaded at the end of the nineteenth century. Over the next fifteen years they bought more land, eventually totaling 2,400 acres. They also planted about 700 acres of vines.

The Denneys are impassioned about everything they do, including the Percheron draft horses they raise. They purchased their first one in 1996, primarily as a "pasture ornament," but fell in love with the "sweet, majestic, wonderful horses." The Denneys have become the largest Percheron breeders in the West and travel with their hitch of black Percheron mares. Their trips promote the Hames Valley wine label, but they also allow the Denneys to bridge the gap between agriculture and modern urban life for those who are long removed from the family farm.

Bob Denney loves to behold the dream he and Shelley have built in the last fifteen years. He relishes his freedom to decide how he's going to live each day within the parameters of weather, climate and projects. And he will always have a project. As Shelley says, above all else, Bob Denney is a builder, in every sense of the word.

Bob and Shelley Denney

Hames Valley Vineyards

P.O. Box 450
Bradley, CA 93426
Phone: 877-800-WINE
Fax: 805-472-9467
email: hvvrhd@earthlink.net
Web site: www.hamesvalley.com
Annual Production: 5000 cases
Winemaker: Christian Roguenant
Winery Owners: Bob and Shelley Denney

Access
Not open for tastings

Wines
Sauvignon blanc, Cabernet Franc, Cabernet Sauvignon, Merlot, Martingale (Viognier/Orange Muscat proprietary blend)

Sales of wine-related items: No

Hames Valley Wine Club
Shipments of two bottles four times a year costing about $50; events and other discounts

Picnics and Programs
Participates in Monterey County Vintners and Growers Association events

Pinnacle peaked . . . winding roads past ghost farms . . . the sun's brilliance shining on vineyards and blinding limestone . . . dotted houses . . . a winery . . . an inn . . . a view of a sea of fog rushing into the valley below . . . scurrying birds and animals in the chaparral . . . solitude . . . a condor soars overhead . . . harshness . . . flinty wines . . . a rising Pinnacle moon

Chalone Vineyard

Chalone Vineyard

P.O. Box 518
Soledad, CA 93960
Phone: 831-678-1717
Fax: 831-678-2742
email:
info@chalonewinegroup.com
Web site:
www.chalonevineyard.com
Annual Production: about 4,500 cases
Winemaker: Dan Karlsen
Winery Owners: The Chalone Wine Group, Ltd.

Access
Tasting Room:
Stonewall Canyon Rd & Hwy 146,
Soledad, CA 93960
Open 11:30–5:00 Sat. and Sun.;
weekdays by appointment

Tastings
No tasting fee
Wines: Chardonnay, Chenin blanc, Pinot blanc, Viognier, Pinot noir, Syrah

Sale of wine-related items? Yes

Chalone Wine Club
Shipments of two wines three to four times a year at $50–$60 a shipment; events; additional discounts of wine and wine merchandise; events

High above the Salinas Valley lies an arid area of chaparral and limestone. To the casual eye, the Gabilan bench land appears inhospitable and good for very little beyond cattle grazing. Yet in 1919, Charles Tamm saw a glimmer of his native Burgundy and planted grape vines, probably the first in Monterey County since the days of mission grapes.

Over the next forty years, the land went through several changes of ownership. Will Silvear planted vineyards on what was to become the Chalone property in 1923, successfully selling grapes at high-end prices to wineries such as the Wente Brothers in Livermore. After Silvear's death, the land was sold to Dr. Edward Liska and John Sigman. By the 1960s, however, the vineyard was in bad shape. The vines were poorly tended and the water shortage was becoming critical.

In 1964 Dick Graff entered the Chalone picture, first as a partner with the current owners, and then as the sole owner in 1969. It was a questionable deal for Graff, because the property had no reliable water source, no telephone and no electricity. Nor was there any money to remedy any of these problems. Nonetheless, Graff struggled through the process, hauling water up from the Salinas Valley and creating his wine with a generator and a prayer.

During the same time period in another area of the country, Phil Woodward received his Masters degree in business from Northwestern University. He eventually went to work for Touche Ross and Company, a large accounting firm. While he knew a lot about business, Phil knew almost nothing about wine. That changed when he took a two-week course in wine tasting.

"I really fell in love with the concept of what wine was," Phil says. Everything is connected to wine — history, economics and everything else that Phil enjoys in his life.

Job changes led him to California, and his interest in wine led him to taste a bottle of 1969 Chalone Pinot blanc. Woodward was hooked and worked all his connections to meet Dick Graff. In 1972, Phil quit his job with Touche and became a partner, along with several other family members, in the Chalone enterprise.

The next twenty years were growth years at Chalone. Woodward helped raise needed funds and Graff continued to create great wine, assisted in the 1980s by Michael Michaud.[1] However, the group needed a significant amount of funds to make the structural changes that were needed, so in 1984, the company went public. Instead of Chalone, Incorporated, it became Chalone Wine Group, Ltd.

Chalone Vineyard winery

The new funds allowed them to make significant changes to the property. In 1984, the company added caves for 3,500 square feet of wine storage. Finally, in 1985, electricity and phones came to Chalone. A year later, the group had acquired water rights and built the infrastructure to transport water seven and a half miles from Soledad. Five pumping stations are used to get the water 1,500 feet up the mountain at 500 gallons a minute.

The 1990s brought many challenges and changes to the company. Over the years it had expanded to include other wineries and investors (most notably Baron Eric de Rothschild). It became a company that was different from the one Graff and Woodward had founded, so in 1996, Dick Graff left the company.[2]

In 1998 Dan Karlsen became Chalone's current winemaker. Tragically, Graff was killed in a small plane accident in January of the same year.

Since that time Karlsen has been involved in revitalizing the vineyard and improving the mechanics of this remote winery. He began with a complete evaluation of the land and climate, as well as the health and appropriateness of the vines (including clones and rootstock) to the soil.

"Soil imparts something to the wine," Karlsen says. "*Terroir* is the flavor of the soil in the wine, not a microclimate." He believes that the limestone soil of Chalone causes the vines to struggle, limiting vigor and bringing a more mineral flavor to the wine.

Within the winery, Karlsen strives for dependability in his wine, believing that the consumer should be able to open a bottle of Chalone wine and know what he or she is getting every time. Along with the rigor required to produce this dependable bottle of wine, he acknowledges that making wine is both a scientific and a hedonistic endeavor. He believes that the primary work of winemaking is done in the vineyard, and that gentle handling of fruit and proper winemaking procedures bring the results that he wants.

Although the winery is remote, no understanding of Monterey wines and their history is complete without a trip up the mountain. There you will find the large limestone rocks that enticed Charles Tamm to

View from Chalone Vineyard tasting room

plant his first vines. You can experience the rugged beauty of the Pinnacles. And you can also taste what Dan Karlsen calls the world's most hedonistic wines.

---

[1] See Michaud Vineyard, page 88.
[2] In December 2004, the Chalone Wine Group signed an agreement with Diageo North America for the acquisition of Chalone by Diageo North America.

Woodward/Graff Wine Foundation

After 32 years of running the Chalone Wine Group,[1] Phil Woodward decided he no longer wanted to continue. Finding a replacement, he ended his tenure as CEO in 1999, and as Chairman of the company in 2001. Phil then turned his attention to enhancing an idea that he'd come up with after the death of Dick Graff, a scholarship that enabled him to give back to the wine business.

Phil Woodward

The Richard H. Graff Scholarship Fund was designed to give money to "people who wanted to continue their education in food or wine or both." The first 10 scholarships were offered in 1998. The scholarships are intended to be used for beginning studies in the wine, food or hospitality fields and include daily living expenses for commuting, parking, day care, etc. The administration of the scholarship selection is done by the Marin Educational Fund.

In 1999, Phil expanded the idea and created the Woodward-Graff Wine Foundation, a wine business, a wine tour business and a way to fund the scholarship fund. Phil says there are three rules to this new business: no employees, no bank debt and no shareholders.

The grapes for the wines that are produced under the Woodward-Graff Wine Foundation name come from three main sources. The first is a small vineyard on the Chalone bench owned by three members of the Graff family (David, John and Peter) and another vineyard that had been owned by Dick Graff before he died, which is now owned by Steven Head from Carmel. Steve sells his grapes to Phil. Another vineyard on the Chalone bench owned by Richard and Carrie Boer supplies grapes for the A-Frame Vineyard label. (Richard is the vineyard manager for Chalone.) A third source is fruit from the Paragon Vineyard in Edna Valley by San Luis Obispo. That wine, Collaboration, is symbolic of a partnership between Chalone and the Paragon Vineyard that goes back to 1977.

All wines are made for the foundation by Chalone Vineyard with the exception of Collaboration, which is made by Paragon's Baileyana Winery.

The foundation enables Phil to stay in the wine business in the Chalone AVA and give back to the business that brought him joy, excitement and satisfaction throughout his life.

---

[1] See Chalone Vineyard, page 84.

Gabilan Cellars

Bill Brosseau grew up between two worlds. The first was the suburban town of Los Altos, California. The second was the rarified atmosphere of the Gabilan Mountains near the Chalone Vineyard. Bill's parents, Jan and Jon, were lured to the mountains after tasting a bottle of Chalone Chenin blanc. They fell in love with the area and bought 160 acres in 1978.

Since they were so close to the Chalone Vineyard, the Brosseaus, with Chalone's encouragement, decided to plant vines. Having grown up around vineyards and winemaking, it was inevitable that Bill studied viticulture and enology at Davis after he graduated from high school. He began to work with the fruit of his parents' vineyard during the harvest of 1997.

The Brosseau Vineyard is littered with large chunks of limestone; the chalky rocks add a surreal moonscape to the land's surface. Until Chalone managed to bring water to the top of the mountain in 1987, the Brosseaus spent a great deal of time moistening the dusty and dry soil with water trucked in from the Salinas Valley. The harsh climate also leads to truly stressed vines and low yields, a benefit to the creation of high-intensity fruit.

Through his Chalone connections, Bill eventually became the winemaker for Testerossa in Los Gatos and has worked for the winery since 2000. By having his own winery as well as working for someone else, he was able to experiment and learn, developing his own unique style. "Rob and Diana Jensen (Testerossa's owners) have been very supportive," Bill says.

A key word in Bill's vocabulary is balance. It's one of the criteria he uses to determine the phenological ripeness that indicates when the fruit is ready to pick. Other factors include the flavor of the grapes and the brix, acid and Ph numbers.

The Brosseaus founded their vineyard on the stalwart grape of Chalone, Chardonnay, and have added Pinot noir and Rhône varietal vines such as Syrah to their vineyard. Bill notes that there's a small bit of Chenin blanc as well, a remembrance of what initially brought the Brosseaus to the Chalone bench land.

Bill thoroughly enjoys the life he has chosen. There's something new every day as he continually fine-tunes his winemaking process to achieve better and better wines. With the evolution of the Chalone area to new varietals and Bill's ever increasing knowledge, there will be plenty to retain his interest.

In the meantime, Jan and Jon Brosseau have turned their property into a delightful and unique bed and breakfast, The Inn at the Pinnacles. A visit to the inn is a great way to experience the life and land that created the winemaker of Gabilan Cellars.

Gabilan Cellars

1638 Randolph Parkway
Los Altos, CA 94024
Phone/Fax: 650-965-0540
email: bbrosseau@earthlink.net
Web site:
www.brosseauvineyards.com
Inn at the Pinnacles web site:
www.innatthepinnacles.com
Annual Production: 125 cases
Winemaker: Bill Brosseau
Winery Owner: Bill Brosseau

Access
Not open for tastings

Wines
Chardonnay, Pinot noir

Bill Brosseau

Michaud Vineyard

Michaud Vineyard

P.O. Box 620163
Woodside, CA 94062-0163
Phone: 650-529-0973
Web site:
www.michaudvineyard.com
Annual Production: 3,000–4,000 cases
Winemaker: Michael Michaud
Winery Owners: Michael Michaud and Carol Hastings

Access
Not open for tastings

Wines
Chardonnay, Pinot blanc, Marsanne, Sangiovese, Pinot noir, Syrah

The Michaud Vineyard sits 1500 feet above the Salinas Valley floor on 267 acres of rolling hills in the Chalone AVA. All is quiet except for the sounds of birds, insects, frogs and the occasional drone of a helicopter or airplane. It's a place that hosts the solitude (only one person per 10 square miles) that owner and winemaker Michael Michaud requires for his peace of mind and his 28-acre vineyard.

When Michael graduated from U.C. Davis in 1979, he accepted a job at Chalone Vineyard as an assistant winemaker to Richard Graff. It took a great deal of self-reliance to accept that offer, rather than take the usual winemaker's position. At that time Chalone Vineyard was "off the grid" — it had no telephone and no dependable supply of running water.[1]

In spite of the difficulties, Michael immediately connected with the land and climate, as well as their expression in the grapes and wine of the area. He was so taken by the experience, that he purchased ten acres and a decrepit house in the Gabilan Mountains in 1980, followed by the purchase of 40 more acres in 1982 and 217 additional acres in 1984.

Like the land that Chalone farms, Michael's property has significant pockets of granite and limestone, providing good drainage for the 12 to 15 inches of annual rainfall in the high desert land. There are six to twelve inches of what Michael jokingly refers to as "top soil." Much of the earth is decomposed granite and clay loam surrounding the granite boulders and limestone that break through the surface. As difficult as the land can be to farm, the soil supplies a minerality that provides a unique characteristic to Chalone AVA wines.

In 1981 Michael planted his first vineyard block of Pinot blanc grape vine cuttings from the 1946 Chalone planting. The vineyard is close to the house, now somewhat remodeled. Over 20 years later, the unfenced vines are thriving, although for a time Michael was plagued by "pinot-loving pigs." The problem was solved, ironically, with bird netting.

Happy in his isolation, Michael was married to the land and considered the vines his extended family — until he met his future wife, Carol Hastings, in 1984. Their marriage in 1989 and the birth of their son, Jamie, in 1991 pulled Michael out of his vineyard isolation. Since then he's relied on his vineyard manager, Edrulfo Agustin, for day-to-day work, but Michael gets up to the mountain as often as possible.

Michael left Chalone Vineyard in 1998 in order to pay closer attention to his own vineyard and winemaking. He invites you to enjoy the results of that work and consider his wine "a consumable artwork and weather record of a particular year."

---

[1] See Chalone Vineyard, page 84.

Michael Michaud

Giant sand dunes frame the glistening bay . . . otters frolic in the aquarium . . . children tentatively touch tentacles . . . high-end stores and restaurants beckon those who emerge from 17 Mile Drive . . . the great flood plains of the Salinas River . . . Santa Lucia Mountains hide the sea . . . Gabilan Mountains contain the valley's eastern end . . . wheels cluck down Highway 101 . . . Steinbeck Country . . . Salinas celebrates land and man . . . tractors, pipes, sprays in the wind . . . Chualar, Gonzales, Soledad, Greenfield, King City, San Lucas, San Ardo . . . footsteps of Native Americans, missionaries, soldiers . . . El Camino Real . . . wind driven fog . . . vineyards

Banyan Wines

With two generations in the wine business, the father and son team of Somchai and Kenny Likitprakong knew the kind of fruit they wanted in order to produce their wines. They also knew the kinds of wines they wanted to produce — wines that would add an extra dimension to the foods that Somchai Likitprakong grew up with in his native Bangkok. In 2003 the pair began their effort to create the best wines possible for Thai cuisine.

As is the case with most new business owners, both Somchai and Kenny have "day jobs." Somchai is president and CEO of Domaine St. Georges near Healdsburg in Sonoma County, a company he joined in 1973. Kenny is the winemaker for Hallcrest Vineyards/Organic Wine Works in Felton, California.[1] Both are dedicated to obtaining fruit from growers who farm responsibly.

When they began to seek out sources for the types of wines they wanted to make, the Likitprakongs realized that only Mendocino and Monterey Counties could provide what they needed. The logistics pointed to Monterey County. In addition to some organic farmers, there is also a large effort to maintain sustainable farming, supported by a point system developed by the Central Coast Vineyard Team.[2] Monterey also had the best climates for the grape varieties the Likitprakongs wanted to use: Gewürztraminer, Riesling and Viognier.

Kenny makes his decision to pick based primarily on flavor, but he also is concerned about losing acid, particularly with Gewürztraminer. According to Kenny, Gewürztraminer holds acid really well, and then drops quickly; he has a three-day window to pick to get the grapes he wants.

Once the fruit is picked, Kenny whole-cluster presses the Gewürztraminer and Riesling. His Gewürztraminer is 90% tank fermented and 10% barrel fermented. The Riesling is all barrel fermented to promote a dry style.

The Likitprakongs' objective is to have a wine that is refreshing and easy to drink without being overly expensive. They are primarily selling to Asian restaurants and markets, but admit it can be a tough sell. Many Asians don't drink wine, and their customers gravitate towards Chardonnay and Merlot, wines which do not particularly enhance Asian foods.

Banyan wines reflect the Likitprakongs' heritage. Their labels, designed by another father and son team, incorporate longboats used in Thailand. The name itself is a remembrance of the Asian banyan tree, which is said to house spirits and possess great beauty and strength.

The next time you are in an Asian restaurant, bypass the Merlot and Chardonnay in favor of varietal wines created by Kenny and Somchai that are designed to enhance the flavors of your food.

---

[1] For more information on Hallcrest Vineyards/Organic Wine Works, see *Mountain Vines, Mountain Wines.*
[2] See McIntyre Vineyards, page 104.

Banyan Wines

604-B 2nd St.
Santa Cruz, CA 95060
Phone/Fax: 831-459-0468
email: info@banyanwines.com
Web site: www.banyanwines.com
Annual Production: about 600 cases
Winemaker: Kenny Likitprakong
Winery Owners: Kenny and Somchai Likitprakong, Lynn Wheeler

Access
Not open for tastings

Wines
Gewürztraminer, Riesling, Viognier

Somchai and Kenny Likitprakong

Baywood Cellars

Baywood Cellars

5573 W. Woodbridge Rd.
Lodi, CA 95242
Phone: 209-337-0445
Fax: 209-334-0137
email:
mail@baywood-cellars.com
Web site:
www.baywood-cellars.com
Annual Production: 20,000 cases
Winemaker: John Cotta
Winery Owners: Cotta Family

Access
Tasting Room:
381 Cannery Row, Suite C
Monterey, CA 93940
Phone: 831-645-9035; 800-214-0445
Fax: 831-645-9345
Open 11–8 daily (winter); 11–9 daily (summer)

Tastings
Tasting fee: $1–$3, refundable with purchase
Wines: Chardonnay, Gewürztraminer, Pinot grigio, Symphony, Cabernet Sauvignon, Merlot, Pinot noir, Sangiovese, Syrah, Tempranillo, Zinfandel, port

Club Baywood
Two bottles three to four times a year from $39–$49 per shipment

Sale of wine-related items? Yes

Picnics and Programs
Participates in Monterey County Winegrowers Association events

Recognizing the city of Monterey as a key destination for visitors to the Central Coast, John Cotta opened his tasting room there in 1997 to showcase his Monterey County and Central Coast wines. Enter the tasting room on Cannery Row and you'll immediately notice the warm, friendly atmosphere. As you taste the wines, take time to browse through the photos that hang on the walls, including one of George Azevedo, maternal grandfather of John and James Cotta.

The Cotta family roots stretch back across the Atlantic to Portugal. Although John Cotta, Baywood's winemaker and co-owner, isn't positive that his ancestors made wine, it's probable. Once in the United States, George Azevedo and his three brothers stored illegal wine in their basement, like many recent immigrants from Europe who couldn't understand what all the fuss was about during Prohibition. Unfortunately, George died in 1932, leaving his family to ride out the depression without him.

Another photograph shows St. Bartholomew's Church on the island of Terceira in Portugal.

The church, established in the late 1500s, was the religious home of many of the Cotta family. With this strong Portuguese background from both sides of the family, it's understandable that Baywood Cellars produces a well-recognized port wine.

However, just as the port wine belongs at the end of a meal, it belongs at the end of this story. The beginning takes place near Lodi, California, where the Cotta family has been growing wine grapes and other agricultural commodities for three quarters of a century.

Cotta Properties was founded in 1925 by Joe Cotta Sr. in California's San Joaquin Valley. This valley contains a large part of California's agricultural bounty. The Cotta family has helped create that bounty. Among the agricultural commodities grown by the family were wine grapevines. These were, and still are, sold to other wineries.

John and James Cotta, Joe Senior's grandsons, eventually became part of the family business. A self-confessed rebel, John argued that the family should move beyond the fruit to the beverage. John, a rather persistent fellow, kept voicing his opinions until, in 1985, the family caved in and the Cotta's Las Viñas label made its debut.

Baywood tasting room

John enjoyed his success making the Las Viñas wines, which won Best of Region awards at the California State Fair wine competitions of 1988, 1989 and 1990. However, he felt there was still something missing in the wine he was creating. The flavor he wanted couldn't be made from the grapes the family harvested in Lodi.

Monterey County and the Central Coast provided John with the taste he desired. The climate and soil of this region result in the flavor found in Baywood Cellar's wines. John purchases the best grapes that he can from vineyards that use sustainable practices.

John's winemaking technique includes use of the most modern, state-of-the-art equipment. The Krones filler-corker machines and MEB rotary star labeling equipment allow the winery to bottle up to 150 bottles a minute. However, regardless of the speed with which the bottling takes place, John seeks to create a unique wine, one that carries more fruit essence and intensity than the average wine in the market. His grapes are harvested at night when the air is cool. They go through a full extraction so that the fruit flavor is balanced by the tannins. John doesn't want to produce a wine with a "hollow center," since he believes that the tannins are essential to the flavor. He also avoids a huge infusion of new oak in his barrels, allowing the wood to become a background fragrance that adds complexity to the wine.

John cheerfully admits that he could have invested in the stock market and made more money, but he prefers the challenge of making a good wine known by consumers. He's happy with his Cannery Row tasting room in Monterey. "What do you have to lose?" he says. "You can throw a stone in the ocean from here and eat at a different great restaurant 365 days a year."

The next time you are in Monterey, stop by the tasting room to enjoy some of John Cotta's wine. Be sure to try the wine of his Portuguese heritage (port), produced from vines descended from those smuggled in from Douro, Portugal, by John's great-grandfather.

Winemaking has always been in the Azevedo and Cotta families — even before they emigrated from Portugal. Perhaps they even sold some wine commercially (although in barrels, not in bottles). John hasn't quite made up his mind as to whether keeping up the family tradition is a blessing or a curse.

Of course, you'll need to taste the wines to make up your own mind on that subject.

John Cotta

Blackstone Winery

Blackstone Winery

800 South Alta St.
Gonzales, CA 93926
Phone: 831-675-5341
email: blackstone.info@
blackstonewinery.com
Web site:
www.blackstonewinery.com
Annual Production: 1,000,000+
cases
Winemaker: Dennis Hill
Winery Owners: Constellation
Brands, Inc.

Access
Open 11–4 daily

Tastings
No tasting fee
Wines: Chardonnay, Sauvignon
blanc, Cabernet Sauvignon,
Merlot, Pinot noir, Syrah

Sale of wine-related items? Yes

Picnics and Programs
Picnic area on site; participates
in Monterey County Vintners and
Growers Association events

Traveling on Highway 101 near Gonzales, it's difficult to miss the large monk-brown buildings and giant-sized wine tanks on the west side of the freeway. This is the Blackstone Winery and well worth a turn off the highway to take a look.

The facility dates back to the 1970s, when it produced wine for Monterey Vineyards, a winery started at that time by a land trust.[1] The building was subsequently sold to Coca-Cola for their Taylor California Cellars brand. In October 2001 it became home to Blackstone Winery.

In 2001 Blackstone became part of Pacific Wine Partners, a joint venture created that same year by Constellation Brands, Inc. and BRL Hardy Ltd., an Australian company. In 2003, Pacific Wine Partners became a wholly owned subsidiary of Constellation Brands, Inc.

Blackstone Winery in Monterey County is the main winemaking facility for Blackstone Wines. In addition to the Monterey facility which is capable of crushing 35,000 tons of grapes a year, Pacific Wine Partners owns 1,400 acres of vineyards in Monterey County, and two other facilities in Sonoma and Mendocino Counties. The Monterey facility continues to produce the

Blackstone tasting room

Blackstone Winery was a "virtual" winery when Derek and Courtney Benham began it in 1990. The two California natives graduated from Berkeley in the early 1980s and worked for Barengo Winery during that decade. They started Blackstone as one of the many private and control labels that they produced. With the increasing popularity of Merlot in the 1990s, the Benhams decided to focus on that varietal wine with Blackstone. In 1994, Dennis Hill joined them to help perfect their Merlot wine. Their business model was unique to the wine industry at that time. They didn't own a winemaking facility for many years. Instead they contracted with various winemaking facilities to do crushing, fermenting, aging and bottling under their direction. Seven years after they began, Blackstone's Merlot had become the most popular in the country.

California Merlot which began the Blackstone Winery, as well as Chardonnay and Pinot noir wines created from grapes grown on the Santa Lucia Highlands.

Winemaker Dennis Hill stayed on when the winery changed hands; he now leads a team of winemakers, each focused on their own special contributions to Blackstone Wines.

Like many others, Dennis didn't intend to become a winemaker when he set out studying art and design at San Jose State. However, he was lured into the wine business in 1973 when he accepted an offer from his landlord to help with the "crush." He fell in love with the wonderful complexity and sensory beauty of fine wines. That inspiration motivated him to study chemistry and enology at U.C. Davis. He began his true occupation at the Seghesio Winery,

Alexander Valley Vineyards and deLorimier Winery in Sonoma County. In the late 1970s, Dennis traveled to Europe to expand his wine-tasting horizons beyond the California palate.

Dennis Hill likes Merlot because it is a versatile wine that goes with many foods and appeals to everyone who drinks red wine. His affection for the grape let him to Mill Creek Winery in 1989 where he focused on producing an outstanding Merlot. His efforts won him the Louis Benoist Award for Winemaking. In 1994 Dennis's Merlot quest led him to Codera Wine Group and the focus on Blackstone Winery.

Vineyard cultivation is important to Dennis since he believes that the quality of the grapes has an enormous impact on the quality of the wines produced. He works closely with growers, enjoying their relationships as well as the opportunity to influence their growing practices. He asks them to consider which course of agriculture will create the least impact on the environment over the long term at every decision point in the grape-growing process. To maximize the flavors of the wine, Dennis bases his harvest date on the developed flavor of the grapes, not just on the numbers.

The grapes that go into Monterey County wines are primarily machine-picked, which is true of most vineyards in Monterey. Dennis tries to get the fruit at its coolest, which means starting before the sun rises in the morning.

Dennis achieves a balance in his wines so that they taste fruit-forward and never harsh. He uses different techniques from cold soaking to earlier pressing of grapes to maximize flavor and eliminate any hard tannins that may come from the seeds of the grapes.

Dennis Hill is optimistic about Monterey County's future in agriculture, including viticulture. He sees that the county is interested in preserving its agricultural heritage, not breaking up farms for houses.

After you pull off the whizzing highway, you'll find a pleasant drive through green lawns and swaying eucalyptus trees to the tasting room. If you bring a picnic lunch, you can enjoy it over-looking a serene pond, shaded by more trees. You will, however, need to negotiate with the geese who will demand their tribute. Fortunately, they won't be interested in your Blackstone Merlot.

---

[1] See the history chapter for more information.

Dennis Hill

Boyer Wines

Boyer Wines

P.O. Box 7267
Spreckels, CA 93962-7267
Phone: 831-455-1885
Fax: 831-455-8019
email: boyerwine@aol.com
Annual Production: about 3,000 cases
Winemaker: Rick Boyer
Winery Owner: Rick Boyer

Access
Fri. - Sun. 11-5

Tastings
Tasting Room:
655 River Rd.
Salinas, CA 93908
No tasting fee

Wines
Chardonnay, Gewürztraminer, Riesling, Pinot noir, Syrah

Rick Boyer hadn't planned to become a winemaker. He was attending U.C. Davis, studying agriculture and playing sports, when he discovered that he needed more credits to graduate. His roommate, a young man from Modesto, was taking beginning grape growing and Rick signed up for the course as well.

About the same time, Rick began to date a woman from Sonoma. Together they went to the old Buena Vista Winery tucked in a cave just east of Sonoma. The smell of the old wines emanating from the cave walls added luster to the Gewürztraminer and Riesling that Rick tasted. Learning that the wine business offered a number of different opportunities to work outside and be creative, Rick knew he had found his life's work.

Rick began his work by buying grapes for Gallo in Fresno in 1979. Desiring a smaller operation, Rick joined Ventana Vineyards in 1983 and stayed there for 11 years. In 1985 he started his own winery.

Rick buys grapes from two different buyers for his wines, producing Chardonnay, Pinot noir and small lots of Syrah that are designed to be food-friendly. Boyer Wines are created to be fruit forward with a relatively high acidity and less wood than is found in many California wines. Rick strives to capture a sense of place in his wines through minimal processing. He feels that the job of the winemaker is to be the "guardian of the flavor of the grape." He feels the more changes you make to the wine in the winery, the further away you get from the pure flavor of the *terroir* of the grape.

For his Boyer Wines, Rick uses all French oak barrels because he likes the style that they impart to the wine. To gain more neutrality, he uses two- to three-year-old barrels that are well-maintained, rather than introducing new wood on a yearly basis, as many wineries do.

In 1994, Rick Boyer left Ventana Vineyards to join Jekel Vineyards as Winemaker and General Manager, creating the team that resurrected the winery. As the Jekel business grew, so did Rick's passion for all things natural. The vineyards were converted to organic culture; the land in and around the vineyards came alive with flowers and plants that attracted beneficial insects and provided nutrients for the vines.

The wines changed to reflect the "sense of place" of the organic Greenfield vineyards. Throughout his stay at Jekel, the Boyer label was maintained and refined, allowing Rick to continue to develop his own style, yet create wines for Jekel that spoke of that brand. It was at Jekel that Rick developed a deep appreciation and understanding of the value of organic vineyards. Unfortunately, the Jekel operation closed in January 2004.

Rick feels that wines should be balanced, with fruit as the focal point. With Boyer Wines, he will continue his pursuit of "perfect balance." In following his heart, Rick feels that he is truly fortunate to have found a career that allows him to combine creativity, business skills, and a passion for teaching.

Rick Boyer

Carmichael Wine Company

Michael Leven attributes his love of wine to a stint he served as a waiter in the late 1980s while attending the University of Washington to study economics. The bar manager was very aggressive about serving wine and educated the waiters in the restaurant on pairing food and wine so they would know the correct wine to recommend. The more Michael learned, the less he realized he knew. He became a wine-student for life.

After some time working with his family's business (a professional car racing team), Michael realized that he wanted to run a winery. His wife, Carmen, pointed out that he should probably go back to school to learn to make the stuff first. So off he went to Fresno State University.

Following graduation in 1991, Michael began making wine for a rather large operation — making all the non-varietal white wines for the Glen Ellen Winery, about a million and a half gallons of wine a year. It was there, and later at other large facilities such as Heublein's BV Coastal and Kendall-Jackson, that Michael honed what he considers his greatest strength — blending. He found it imperative to be creative and open-minded as a blender in order to create the best wine possible from grapes culled from many various vineyards and blocks within vineyards.

In 1994 Michael began to develop his own wine under the Carmichael label (a combination of his and his wife's first names). He began with the Sangiovese because he enjoys Tuscan wines, and because he doesn't have to compete against larger operations, which are more likely to concentrate on the popular varietal wines like Merlot and Chardonnay.

Michael sources most of his fruit from Monterey, getting his Pinot blanc, Pinot grigio, Syrah and Sangiovese from Arroyo Seco. More Sangiovese and Cabernet Sauvignon come from San Lucas, and the Syrah comes from the mountains north of King City. Not only does he believe that the fruit is the best that he can get, but he also finds that the winery owners in Monterey county are passionate about what they do. They haven't inherited a family tradition, but are building their own.

About seven or eight years ago, Michael's best friend came to him and said he was the only person he knew that actually made a product that you could hold in your hands. Michael finds himself remembering that sentiment at the end of every year when he reflects on the wine he's made.

Michael Leven

Carmichael Wine Company

1070 Button Court
Turlock, CA 95382
Phone/Fax: 831-214-7736
email: info@carmichaelwine.com
Web site:
www.carmichaelwine.com
Annual Production: about 1,500 cases
Winemaker: Michael Leven
Winery Owner: Michael Leven

Access
Not open for tastings

Wines
Sangiovese (small lots), Grigio e Bianco (white blend of Pinot grigio and Pinot blanc), Sa Vini (a red blend of Sangiovese, Syrah and Cabernet Sauvignon), Sur le Pont (red blend of Syrah, Mourvèdre, Carignan, Grenache)

Picnics and Programs
Participates in Monterey County Vintners and Growers Association events

Caviglia Vineyards

Caviglia Vineyards

63008 Bernardo Road
San Ardo, CA 93450
Phone: (408) 427-2775
email:
clint@cavigliavineyards.com
Web site:
www.cavigliavineyards.com
Annual Production: 800 cases
Winemaker: Clint Marsh
Winery Owners: Clint and Stacey
Marsh

Access
Open 10–5 daily except major
holidays

Tastings
Tasting fee: $3
Wines: Chardonnay, Sauvignon
blanc, Barbera, Pinot noir,
Sangiovese, Zinfandel

Sale of wine-related items? Yes

Caviglia Wine Club
Two bottles monthly for about
$40 per shipment; member-only
events

Picnics and Programs
Holds various events throughout
the year

Dreams of how we want our lives to be are often formed when we're small, enjoying times with our families. Such was the case for Clint Marsh. His memories go back to his Italian immigrant grandfather, Andrew Caviglia, who passed away in Los Altos in 1985. Clint remembers making wine with his Nono (Italian name for grandpa), using the same barrels that his great-grandfather had coopered. According to Clint, "Sometimes the wine was good; sometimes not so good."

Clint carried this dream through his early life in a very different business. He received his economics degree from San Diego State University in 1994 and started his career in international industrial sales. He found money and stress to be the cornerstone of heavy equipment sales. Everyone was working to cut costs in any manner possible. Always, the memory of his grandfather's winemaking tickled his imagination.

At this time Clint was living in the Santa Clara Valley (also known as Silicon Valley) and he began to notice that there were a great many old neglected vineyards in the area.[1] To provide contrast to his sales life, Chris began to care for the vineyards, learning a great deal about viticulture along the way. Two of the vineyards he worked included a field of Petite Syrah on Watsonville Road and a 75-year-old head-pruned Carignan vineyard near the Solis Vineyard on Route 152 — both near Hecker Pass.

Working with the vineyards allowed Clint to become part of the local winery community. He learned from winemakers at Fortino, Thomas Kruse and George Guglielmo, among others. But his greatest resource was Alan Kruetzer of Kirigin Cellars. In 2000 Clint started making his own wine.

As he worked the vines, Clint's life dream resurfaced and he began to wonder if he could actually make a living in the wine business.

It's often said that when we are open to an opportunity, one will appear. On the way back home from his brother's wedding in 2003, Clint and his new wife, Stacey, passed a winery for rent on Highway 101.

Clint and Stacey Marsh

Wineries for rent are not a common sight in Monterey County — especially wineries complete with use permits and tasting room facilities. John and Dorothy Bamford, the property owners, are retired Nob Hill Grocery employees. They felt that a winery/tasting room was the perfect addition to their land near Highway 101. They did all the work to acquire the permits needed, which was a good stroke of luck for the Marshes. The Bamfords and Marshes made a deal and Stacey and Clint went to work.

The Marshes planned, painted and bought, creating an inviting way station by the thundering rush of the cars on Highway 101. Clint brought some of his grandfather's equipment into the tasting room. He had hoped to use it for winemaking, but found it didn't work quite as well as it used to. On July 4, 2004, the tasting room opened for business.

Clint believes that you can't make a good wine with bad fruit; therefore, he spends a great deal of time in the vineyard, working with the plants. He prunes very aggressively, leaving three canes with two buds per cane which results in low-yield, high-quality fruit. Clint's a great fan of organic fruit, although he believes that true organic wine is difficult to bring to market. He avoids the use of pesticides, but sulfur is necessary to prevent mildew on plants to keep them from rotting.

Clint's ideal wine is one that presents the fruit of the vine in a glass. He achieves this by caring for the fruit in the vineyard and doing as little adjustment as possible in the winery. To create the taste he wants in his wines, Clint prefers blending different lots of wine together.

In terms of the winemaking process, Clint ferments at a higher temperature than most. He uses one- to two-year-old French barrels whenever possible, believing that the purpose of the barrel is to soften the wine, not make it taste like oak.

The winemaking lifestyle appeals to Clint, as it does to many others, because of the variety of work that's required and the number of nice people he gets to deal with. He remembers helping his Nono when he was young (although he admits he was probably more of a pain from his grandfather's point of view). The memories include little squat glasses of wine on the table while his grandfather and friends played cards after the work was done. This legacy has led Clint to believe that winemaking is as much a social experience as an industrial project, and he's glad to be involved.

Clint and Stacey invite you to stop on your way to somewhere else, "take a load off," and enjoy the bounty of the winemaking experience.

---

[1] For more information on these vineyards, see *Like Modern Edens*, by Charles Sullivan.

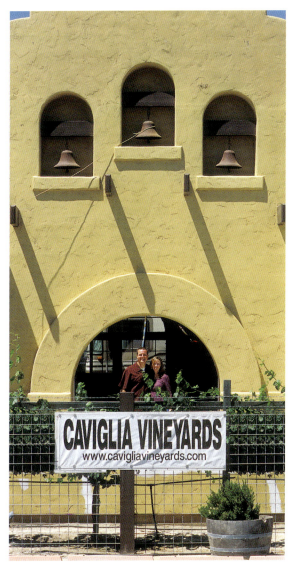

Caviglia tasting room

de Tierra Vineyards and Winery

de Tierra Vineyards and Winery

P.O. Box 3737
Salinas, CA 93912
Phone: 831-484-2557
Fax: 831-484-7932
Annual Production: about 400 cases
Winemaker: Tom Russell
Winery Owners: Tom and Carol Russell and Lucio Gomiero

Access
Not open for tastings

Wines
Merlot, Syrah

Picnics and Programs
Picnic area on site; participates in Monterey County Vintners and Growers Association events

Tucked up a winding road between the Santa Lucia Highlands and Carmel Valley, lies a sheltered valley that John Steinbeck called the "pastures of heaven." It was once discovered by Spanish missionaries who were looking for a good place to graze cattle. The missionaries built an earthen dam to contain water from the stream that flowed through the valley, and to hold in the cattle. The valley was called Corral de Tierra (corral of earth); it's from this origin that de Tierra Vineyards and Winery takes its name.

In the mid-1990s, Carol and Tom Russell bought a piece of property in this valley; they felt it would be the perfect place to grow Merlot, as well as build a home and winery. The Russells purchased 20 acres, including a south-facing bowl with a six to eight degree slope, and a microclimate that was different from the fog-strewn climate of northern Monterey County. In 1997 they began to prepare the soil and design the vineyard with the help of a close friend and co-owner, Lucio Gomiero (a vintner from the Veneto region of Italy).

The same care and control that the Russells put into creating the vineyard goes into maintaining it. Crop yield is kept to an average of two and a half to three tons per acre because the vineyard is pruned to leave only six or seven canes per plant and allow one grape cluster per cane. The care continues during harvest when the grapes are hand-picked into buckets and then crushed, de-stemmed and fermented in the winery on the property. There, the wine is allowed to age in Hungarian oak barrels for 12 months.

Although de Tierra is a fairly young winery, they have standards in place to insure that they control every facet of each varietal wine they make, from picking the clone and root stock for the vine to crushing and pressing the grapes to insure that they produce top quality wine.

de Tierra Vineyards and Winery

In addition to the vineyard and winery, Tom owns one of the largest organic farming businesses in California, Pure Pacific Organics. He has put the practices he's used in the produce business to work on his vineyard land. As a result, the vineyard was the first one to be certified organic by the California Certified Organic Farmers (CCOF); the vineyard shares its space with owls, bats and ladybugs.

Estancia Estates

As a company, Estancia Estates had its beginnings in the Alexander Valley of Sonoma County. Agustin Huneeus established Estancia soon after becoming president of Franciscan Estates; he wanted to find the best place to grow Chardonnay, since the grape was ill-suited to the Alexander Valley. Huneeus found that Monterey County had all the characteristics of a world-class Chardonnay-producing area. In 1998 he purchased the 900-acre Pinnacles Vineyard near Soledad, as well as some of the winery buildings. Both had been part of the Monterey operation of the Paul Masson Winery; the other winery buildings were sold to Golden State Vineyards.[1]

With Howard Tugael, the vineyard manager, Huneeus determined which Chardonnay and Pinot noir clones and rootstock worked best for the microclimate on the bench land above the east side of the Salinas Valley. Over the next 10 years the winery expanded its holdings to an additional 300 acres by the Pinnacles site, and a 100-acre vineyard on the Santa Lucia Highlands. Currently, there are 1,400 acres in Monterey that are owned by Estancia, 990 acres of which are under vine.

Although the size of the Estancia winery is significant, the philosophy of the winery owners and that of their winemakers has focused on treating the wine as if it were being made in small wineries. Estancia believes that the wine should reflect the "somewhereness" of its origin, "so that each of our wines reflects the full expression of our vineyards."

Estancia has been blessed with creative winemakers since its origin, including Dan Karlsen (now at Chalone) and Ken Shyvers (now at Blackstone). The position of head winemaker was open at the time of this writing, but Robert Cook oversees production of the red wine and Chris Todd oversees production of the white wine.

Both Robert and Chris have experience working with small wineries, and they carry the old-world techniques they learned at their previous jobs into the large winery of Estancia. Those techniques include insuring that the winemaking equipment at Estancia can handle the fruit properly, yet at the pace needed to insure that the huge amounts of fruit get processed rapidly. For example, Pinot noir grapes are either hand-picked or machine-picked in such a way that it is often gentler than hand-picking. Pinot noir grapes are never put into tanks using a must pump. A membrane press, a relatively new machine which looks like an old fashioned hand-press with a computer, is being put to use to create the effect of the old world with the speed of the new for white grapes, as well as some Merlot and Cabernet Sauvignon grapes.

The aim of Estancia is to produce a quality wine from estate vineyards at a reasonable price. Robert refers to the technique as making old world wine on a new-world scale. They hope that the next time you choose a wine for dinner, you try an Estancia wine. They believe you will go back for more.

---

[1] See Golden State Vintners, page 103.

Estancia Estates

1775 Metz Rd.
Soledad, CA 93960
Phone: 831-678-7008
Fax: 831-678-7090
email: winemaker@estanciaestates.com
Web site:
www.estanciaestates.com
Annual Production: 600,000+ cases
Winemakers: Chris Todd and Robert Cook
Winery Owners: Franciscan Estates (A Constellation Company)

Access
Not open for tastings

Wines
Chardonnay, Pinot grigio, Cabernet Sauvignon, Merlot, Pinot noir, Zinfandel, Meritage (a red Bordeaux-style blend)

Expressions of *Terroir* Wine Club
Shipments of two bottles monthly from the entire Franciscan line of wines

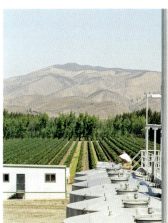

Robert Cook

Faun Vineyards

Faun Vineyards

San Lucas, CA
Web site: faunvineyards.com
Annual Production: about 700 cases
Winemaker: J.D. Agular
Winery Owner: J.D. Agular

Access
Not open for tastings

Wines
Chardonnay, Pinot noir, Syrah, port

Driving through the Salinas Valley some evening, you might be startled by eerie lights bobbing among the grapevines. It's probably nothing to worry about — only J.D. Agular and his fellow pickers in their miners' helmets. J.D. picks at night to insure that his fruit is chilled, retaining the flavor and ripeness that he desires for Faun wines. And he hand picks all his fruit — hence the miners' helmets.

J.D. has the winemaker's reverence for making truly "hand-crafted" wines whenever possible. Faun had its beginnings in J.D.'s home, when he and his brother-in-law made a couple of barrels of wine a year. They wound up giving most of it away, but their friends insisted that they should move into the commercial arena.

A combination of many factors brought J.D. to the Salinas Valley from his native San Diego. The first was a woman — he'd met Ginger (a southern California native who was living in Salinas) at a wedding in San Diego and began making the commute to visit her. (The two married in 2003.) When in the Salinas Valley, J.D. was impressed with both the friendliness of the people and the similarity of the climate to that of Napa Valley. He knew it was where he wanted to be.

J.D. took classes from U.C. Davis Extension, but credits training from others in the valley, especially the people at Lockwood Vineyards, for their true understanding of winemaking and the winery business. J.D. is an individualist and committed to making wine to his taste, regardless of current market trends.

Although he currently has no vineyard of his own, J.D. is able to find small blocks of grapes throughout the valley. He carefully selects the fruit he wants, leaving non-approved grapes on the vine.

J.D.'s selectivity extends through the winemaking process. He hand-, or rather foot-, crushes his grapes when it's feasible. J.D. admits he's become quite efficient at stomping grapes, feeling that he's at one with the fruit. He doesn't use sulfur at the beginning of the winemaking process because it interferes with the color he's trying to achieve in the wine.

The rest of J.D.'s wine-making philosophy is ever-evolving. He regards the process as a "lot of fiddling and a lot of science." He's followed what he calls "tangents" over the years, experimenting with different woods and filtering techniques. Now he's moved towards a balanced approach. "Just keep it in the middle and let it go," he says, "and let whatever happens, happen." The result is as much a surprise to him as anyone else. While he finds it sometimes difficult to exactly duplicate a wine exactly, he believes his wines are consistent from year to year.

So grab a bottle of Faun wine and head to your favorite place to have some fun. As J.D. would say, "Life's short, have Faun!"

J.D. Agular

Golden State Vintners (Monthaven Winery)

Driving through Soledad on your way to Chalone, you might notice a large winery facility on the left covering 20 acres. Across from it, another 54 acres of vineyards extend into the distance. Very few cars are in the winery parking lot, because, except for harvest, only around 35 people tend the wine process. Buddy Masuda, former senior winemaker, says that the process works because they "excel at being able to work as a cohesive organism."

While you might assume that the facility is merely for bulk wine; that is not the case. At Golden State Vintners, it's almost as if there are a dozen small wineries going full time, as well as the larger winery operations. The heart of the facility is a computer system that keeps track of time and tanks. The system is based on a huge wall chart developed in the 1980s.

Many small wineries don't have the facilities they need to produce their wine. That's where places like Monthaven Winery come in. They provide outsourcing services for wine processing, including custom crushing, barrel fermentation, barrel storage and aging, and tank storage. Two huge temperature- and humidity-controlled warehouses are stocked floor to ceiling with about 32,000 barrels. Each barrel, as well as each tank, is labeled for identification. That way, a customer can walk in and know exactly where his or her wine is.

At the same time that they are providing wine processing operations for small vintners, the team at Monthaven Winery is producing wine according to specifications for premium wine companies. Golden State Vintners has made a name for itself as being one of the state's leading exporters of California wine to foreign countries. The team also produces the wine for the Monthaven Coastal brand. Their goal is to provide a wine that is easy to drink and enjoy and "makes you happy you swallowed." While you can put Monthaven Coastal away for a year, it is designed for the average wine buyer who drinks the wine the same day it's purchased.

Monthaven Winery is one of four wineries owned by Golden State Vintners (GSV). GSV can trace its roots back to Arpaxat Setrakian who started it at the family's California Growers Winery in Cutler in 1936. As the company grew, it bought and sold other companies and eventually acquired the Monthaven Winery facility (built in 1966) which had originally been part of Seagram's Paul Masson holdings.[1] One of the more interesting remnants from that time is the pink and purple steel walls within one of the original buildings.

Although it is a large company, the people who work for Golden State Vintners have a lot of variation within their jobs and the people they work with. As Georgetta Dane, a Rumanian immigrant and assistant winemaker, says, "I can say for sure it is not boring here."[2]

Golden State fermentation tanks

[1] See the history chapter for more information.
[2] The Wine Group, LLC, purchased the bulk of Golden State Vintners in July 2004.

Golden State Vintners (Monthaven Winery)

1777 Metz Rd.
Soledad, CA 93960
Phone: 831-678-3991
Fax: 831-678-2172
email: mhc@gsvwine.com
Web site:
www.monthavencoastal.com
Capacity: 9.5 million gallons
Senior Winemaker: John P. Clark
Winery Owner: The Wine Group, LLC

Access
Not open for tastings

Wines
Chardonnay, Muscat, Pinot grigio, Sauvignon blanc, Viognier, Cabernet Franc, Cabernet Sauvignon, Malbec, Merlot, Petite Syrah, Petite Verdot, Pinot noir, Syrah, Zinfandel, White Zinfandel

McIntyre Vineyards

McIntyre Vineyards

40410 Arroyo Seco Rd.
Soledad, CA 93960
Phone: 831-678-4845
Fax: 831-678-4846
Annual Production: 1,200 cases
Labels: McIntyre Vineyards,
L'Homme Qui Ris
Winemaker: Steve McIntyre
Winery Owners: Steve and
Kimberly McIntyre

Access
Not open for tastings

Wines
Chardonnay, Merlot, Pinot noir

Steve McIntyre has been a significant figure in the Monterey vineyard and winery establishment since the 1980s. He began by planting vineyards at Galante Vineyards in 1982 and moved to Hahn Estates/Smith and Hook where he was an assistant winemaker for nine years. In 1993, he established Monterey Pacific, a vineyard management company. The company manages about 7,000 acres of vines, some of which are owned by Monterey Pacific.

The out of doors holds a great lure for Steve. He loves being outside, watching the seasons progress, knowing that nothing is ever the same from year to year. The harvest brings a satisfying sense of closure to the year. His appreciation for the land and farming has moved him to join the Central Coast Vineyard Team, an organization that is dedicated to "promoting environmentally and economically sustainable vineyard practices on the Central Coast." The group has come up with a notion of a "Positive Points System (PPS)" to evaluate a vineyard in terms of sustainable practices being used in six categories: pest management, soil management, water management, viticultural management, wine quality and continuing education. These are practices that Steve uses throughout the vineyards that he manages.

In 1998 Steve decided to put his masters degree in enology from Fresno State University to good use, and created the first vintage of McIntyre wine. He believes that the work that he does in the vineyard, for example, managing sustainability, working with new clones, experimenting with trellis systems and managing the canopy, has a significant effect on the wine that he and others make. Because he has access to various vineyards, he can cherry pick from all of those acres to showcase the best grapes. He also has the luxury of putting out wines that aren't in any way substandard because he isn't dependent on a single vineyard for his fruit.

Steve is also a hungry learner and likes to understand and use new technologies where they are appropriate, yet not lose the essence of old world techniques. In 2001, he and other partners established the Monterey Wine Company, LLC, which has a state-of-the-art facility in King City. While the company embraces new techniques such as a pulse air cap management system that uses a large air bubble to break up the wine cap during tank fermentation, the company also a maintains a deep respect for the art of winemaking.

What Steve likes best about winemaking is creating something that will be around after he is gone. It isn't only McIntyre wines that Steve is creating, but a philosophy and viewpoint on Monterey County viticulture and enology that has a tremendous impact on the people and wineries around him.

Steve McIntyre

Parkfield Vineyard

At the southern tip of Monterey County, sitting on top of the San Andreas Fault, lies Parkfield, population 37. Its nickname is the "Earthquake Capital of the World," because the area receives a substantial earthquake (an average magnitude of 6 or so) about every 22 years; the latest occurred in 2004. According to the National Earthquake Prediction Evaluation Council, "Parkfield remains the best identified locale to trap an earthquake." The town is a mixture of U.S. Geological Survey scientists, large-parcel ranchers and a vineyard.

The Miller family has called Parkfield home since 1908, purchasing the land that contains the Parkfield Vineyard in 1935 to raise cattle. As time evolved, so did the Millers. They went from cattle ranching to grain farming. When the grain market started to play out about 10 years ago, the Millers, farmers at heart, looked around for something else to grow. After doing some research, they found they had a good place to grow grape vines, particularly such warm-climate varietal grapes as Cabernet Sauvignon and Zinfandel. These grapes are more difficult to grow in northern Monterey County. In contrast, it's not a good place to grow Chardonnay, so the Millers purchase this varietal grape from other sources.

The Millers believe that the climate in Parkfield sets them apart from many of the other Monterey County vineyards. While they have similar large temperature swings, going from 45 to 100 degrees and back to 45 degrees in a single day, the average temperature is higher than that of the valley. They only have 20 inches of rain annually, which helps them retain control over how much water the vines receive through drip irrigation.

The Millers planted the 170-acre vineyard on flat terrain at an altitude of 1,500 feet in 1995. It's an east-west facing vineyard with rows that are 11 feet apart, with seven and a half feet between each plant. The immaculate vineyard butts up against San Luis Obispo County — merely stepping over a fence will get you there.

The Millers had their first harvest in 1998, creating some wine for themselves, but primarily growing grapes for other people. In 1999 they had their first commercial wine, created by Jon

Parkfield Vineyard tasting room

Brian Bengard

Alexander Hills. In 2004 Jon Korecki became their winemaker; Jon is also winemaker for Madison Cellars. Jon's educational experience includes California Polytechnic Institute and U.C. Davis; in addition he has had over ten years of experience in the wine industry.

The small team at Parkfield consists of the Millers, Korecki and one of the owners of the Parkfield Wine and Produce store, Brian Bengard. Brian notes that everyone is working hard and putting in their time at the new winery. The work is challenging — both the physical labor of creating and maintaining a new vineyard, and the other challenges of marketing and selling grapes and wine in a business that was overwhelmed by grapes at the beginning of the 21st century. However, Brian notes, "we're doing it."

The wines are deepening in color as the vineyards mature, and Jon Korecki continues to develop a style devoted to retaining the fruit flavor of the grape as well as the tannin structure, to add complexity to the wine. With a few exceptions, Parkfield wines are estate-grown and -bottled, which helps the owners maintain control over everything.

Since the town of Parkfield itself is over an hour's drive east of Highway 101, Brian and his partner, Billy Brubaker, decided to locate the Parkfield tasting room in the produce store that they opened in 2003 in Paso Robles. It's a convenient stop off of Highway 101, with ample supplies of produce, meats and other food items, and a well-stocked wine merchandise section.

Meanwhile, back at Parkfield Vineyard, the Millers are straightening up from the last earthquake. In addition to tipping over about 300 cases of wine, the September 2004 earthquake damaged five or six of the vineyard buildings, including Harry Miller's home.

The quaking ground has been home to the Millers for over a century, however, and they aren't likely to move soon. They will continue to invest their time, energy and love for the land to grow the best grapes possible for Parkfield wines.

Pelerin Wines

Pelerin Wines

163 Lorimer Street
Salinas, CA 93901
Phone: (831) 422-2338 (Mon.–Fri., 8–5)
email: info@pelerinwines.com
Web site: www.pelerinwines.com
Annual Production: 850 cases
Winemaker: Chris Weidemann
Winery Owners: Chris and Cathy Weidemann

Access
Not open for tastings

Wines
Pinot noir, Syrah, Zinfandel

Stand in the wine section of any grocery, wine or liquor store and you can become overwhelmed by the variety of wine labels, each competing for your attention. Some are designed by marketing gurus; others reflect the ideas of the winery owners. In the case of Pelerin, which means pilgrim in French, the traveler on the label reflects the owners' quest to create their winery from the great fruit of the Santa Lucia Highlands.

This quest started when Chris Weidemann began working in a wine shop in Connecticut. In 1988 he decided to quit his job and leave school in order to explore more fully the value and attachment people have to wine. His search led him to Freemark Abbey Winery in Napa where he worked the 1988 harvest. He enjoyed the process and camaraderie so much that he stayed on to work in the Stonegate Winery cellar.

Like many others before him, Chris went to U.C. Davis. That's where he met his wife and partner, Cathy. He graduated in 1995 and initially worked at Newton Winery in Carneros before becoming an assistant winemaker at Morgan Winery in Salinas in 1998. Chris learned a great deal about the people and opportunities of the Salinas Valley, including the diverse grape sources, during his four years at Morgan. He put all the information together to produce his first vintage in 2002.

As he puts it, Chris is a "serious Syrah lover." Whenever he travels to France, he makes it his business to taste as many different Syrahs as he can. His initial goal was to pay homage to this Rhône varietal grape by creating his first wine in the traditional French manner. In addition to the Syrahs, however, the quality of the Santa Lucia Highlands Pinot noir has also captured his attention and now represents his second passion.

Chris believes that the cornerstone of fine wine is a reliable source of grapes and premier growers. If you don't have that, you can't make good wine. Chris picks his grapes based on flavor; he has a rough idea of the sugar level (brix), but tends to disregard the pH and acid numbers. Then he devotes himself to tender care of the fermentation and subsequent aging process. He stays away from enzymes, packaged tannins, large acid additions and the like. Chris's aim is to let the wine be what it is, expressing the select fruit he has obtained.

The reward is a wine that evokes the end of a long pilgrim's quest: an easy chair by the fire, empty plates, soft words, sweet songs, tall tales and a long life sipping a beautiful wine.

Chris Weidemann

Tudor Wines

Dan and Christian Tudor don't fit the typical image one might have of winemakers. Two cousins with a high sense of adventure, the Tudors are likely to be found jumping out of perfectly good airplanes (otherwise known as sky diving), surfing or skiing when they aren't tending their wine.

Tudor's family tree reaches back to Hvar, a 182-square-mile island off the coast of Croatia, home to fields of lavender and vines. The Tudors immigrated (with many of their relatives) to the town of Delano in the Central Valley in 1917 and promptly developed fields of table grapes. With this heritage, it was inevitable that Dan would become involved in the winery business.

It was Dan's cousin, Louie Lucas, who introduced Dan to the fun of amateur winemaking while Dan was working for him at Tepusquet Vineyards. In 1982 Dan won his first wine award. However, winemaking stayed in the background for Dan until 1997, when his second telecom company crashed. He decided "it was time to do something fun — the hell with making money."

During this same time period, Joe and Tondré Alarid, vegetable farmers in the Salinas Valley, were trying to determine what to do with 1,000 acres they owned in the Santa Lucia Highlands. The land was too steep for row crops, and all the neighbors seemed to be planting grapes. One of the neighbors, Gerald McFarland, who had had experience in the wine business, told Tondré not to worry, that he'd order the vines for them. Since Tondré and his son Joe figured it was just another field of green growing things, they planted the vines McFarland obtained for them, in what they called their "grape fields."

As Dan and his cousin Christian began to search for the ideal *terroir* for their source of grapes, they began to zero in on the fruit coming out of Monterey County, specifically the Santa Lucia Highlands. His final choice was Pinot noir fruit from the Tondré grape fields, as well as fruit from Paraiso Vineyards, Arroyo Seco (also owned by Dan's cousins from Hvar) and Louie Lucas's Pinot noir vineyard in the Santa Maria Valley.

Dan works closely with the grape growers, looking for "happy grapes" and slowly maturing fruit. He and Joe walk through the vineyards together and share dreams of grapes during harvest season. They wait until the grapes are at the perfect pitch of ripeness, competing with bees, wasps and Jake, the grape-loving Labrador, to harvest the fruit for Dan's wine, as well as the Tondré Vineyard wine which Joe has started to make.

The intensity of harvest is great for the adventurer in Dan, but when the 2004 harvest was behind him, he headed off to New Zealand to make Tudor Pinot noir in Martinborough. In the meantime, he invites you to try "one of the best Pinot noirs you've ever had in your life."

Tudor Wines

3905 State St. Suite 7 Box 118
Santa Barbara, CA 93105
Phone: 831-224-2116
Fax: 831-372-2783
Web site: www.tudorwines.com
email: dantudor@tudorwines.com
Annual Production: 1800 cases
Winemaker: Dan Tudor
Winery Owners: Dan and ChristianTudor

Access
Not open for tastings

Wines
Chardonnay, Pinot noir

Joe Alarid and Dan Tudor

Monterey County
Vintners and Growers'
Association (MCVGA)

Rhonda Motil
PO Box 1793
Monterey, CA 93942-1793
Phone: 831-375-9400
Fax: 831-375-1116
Web site:
www.montereywines.org

Monterey County Associations

One of the elements which strengthens a wine-growing region is an active association of winery owners. Monterey County has such an association, the Monterey County Vintners and Growers Association (MCVGA).

The organization was founded in 1973 to promote Monterey County as a premier grape-growing region. The charter members included wineries and vineyards that are still around today, such as J. Lohr, Chalone, Mirassou, Wente and Arroyo Seco Vineyards, as well as some entities that have grown or changed in the intervening years. Durney Vineyard was sold to Heller and Rich Smith of Junction Viticulture now owns Paraiso Vineyards with his family.

Today, over 70 wineries and vineyards constitute the organization. Some of these, such as Thomas Fogerty, have their roots and wineries elsewhere, but have a dedication to the fruit developed within Monterey County. The organization promotes the region throughout North America, raising awareness for the fine fruit and wine available from the county.

For the consumer, the organization has many events that allow Monterey County wineries to introduce themselves. Among these are:

- An annual winemaker celebration in the city of Monterey in the summer. Participants can sample around 40 wines, taste food from local restaurants, sometimes watch

MCVGA Winemaker's Celebration

cooperage demonstrations, dance to a local band and even take a stab at blending their own wine.

- The Great Wine Escape Weekend in the fall. Separately priced offerings include an opening night gala, winemaker dinners, educational seminars, bus tours, self-guided tours, silent auctions and a grand finale that includes special reserve wines and barrel samples.
- Passport Weekend in the winter. Purchase a passport and you can go to the wineries of your choice, sample special foods and participate in other winning events. Winemaker dinners (separately priced) are also held during the weekend.

Another great way to experience Monterey wines is to join the Taste of Monterey. The Taste of Monterey has two main tasting rooms:

- In Monterey near the Monterey Aquarium
- In Salinas near the Steinbeck Museum

You don't need to be a member to enjoy these tasting rooms, although a fee is collected if you aren't a member. Membership brings you two bottles of Monterey wine monthly, as well as the chance to be involved in numerous events.

Taste of Monterey

Cannery Row Bay View Tasting Room
700 Cannery Row, Ste. KK
Monterey, CA 93940
Phones: 831-646-5446 or 888-646-5446

Salinas Wine Cellar and Tasting Room
127 Main Street (in Oldtown Salinas)
Salinas, CA 93901
Phones: 831-751-1980 or 888-646-5446

Web site:

www.tastemonterey.com

Courtesy of Taste of Monterey

Tasting room gift shop — Taste of Monterey, Monterey

Glossary

alternate bond: A winery with a bond that uses that bond at a winery facility that isn't owned by them.

American Viticultural Area (AVA): A geographic area with similar climate, soil and environmental conditions whose boundaries are legalized by the Alcohol and Tobacco Tax and Trade Bureau (TTB).

appellation: Strictly speaking it refers to the French legal division of grape growing areas – *appellation contrôlée*. This division is similar to the American Viticultural Area (AVA) in the United States. However, the word appellation is casually used as a substitute for AVA.

B-cap closure: A closure that is made up of a seal of wax on the top of the cork rather than using foil to cover the neck of the bottle.

bare root vine: A vine that has not been grafted on to a rootstock.

barrel-fermented: A process in which the wine is fermented totally in the barrels, rather than using steel tanks for initial fermentation.

bench grafting (indoor grafting): Process of grafting a cutting (or clone) of a vine to a desired rootstock. The graft is kept indoors for about a year before being planted in the vineyard.

block: A section within a vineyard.

bond: A TTB designation that indicates a winery can ferment grapes, blend and bottle wine legally. This then makes them a bonded winery. Other types of bonds, such as alternate bonds, allow wine to be produced for several wineries at the same facility.

Bordeaux: A region in France noted for particular varietal grapes: Cabernet franc, Cabernet Sauvignon, Malbec, Merlot, Petit Verdot, Sauvignon blanc, and Sémillon. Wines made from these grapes are frequently referred to as "Bordeaux varietal wines."

Brettanomyces (brett): A strain of yeast that can cause wine to acquire a taste that has been described as "wet dog hair." Injection of SO_2 during the winemaking process aids extreme cleanliness in avoiding this problem.

brix: A scale that measures sugar content in grapes.

bud break: The time in the spring when new buds start appearing on vines.

bud wood: Vine grafted on to rootstock.

Burgundy: A region in France (Bourgogne) known for Pinot noir and Chardonnay (white burgundy) grapes. Burgundy was also used as a generic term for California red wines.

cane: The shoot from the main branches of the vine. Canes are pruned in the winter so only a few are left — the number depends on the trellising and pruning methods employed by the vineyard owner.

cap: Skins from red wine which float to the top during fermentation.

***Chaine D'Or* (golden chain):** A phrase, probably coined by Paul Masson, that refers to the east side of the Santa Cruz Mountains, from Woodside to around the Lexington Reservoir near Los Gatos. It is considered a premium grape growing region.

clone: A cutting from a grape vine that has the same genetic makeup as its parent vine.

***clos*:** Fenced-in area enclosing a small vineyard.

cooper: A person who makes barrels.

custom crush: A facility that allows a winemaker without a winery to make wine on its premises.

district: A region within an appellation or AVA.

domaine: A Burgundian term for a collection of vineyard parcels owned by the same person.

enologist: Someone who has studied the science of wine and its creation.

fermentation: The process by which the sugar of the grape is converted to ethyl alcohol and carbon dioxide. This process produces a great deal of heat which winemakers seek to control.

fine: Clarify the wine by using agents such as egg whites or clays to absorb unwanted material.

hang time: The amount of time that the fruit is on the vine from berry formation until the grapes are harvested.

Integrated Pest Management (IPM): A method of controlling insects, weeds, and other things detrimental to fruit and vegetable development using natural predators.

maceration: Steeping crushed grapes with their skins.

malolactic (ML) fermentation: Transformation of malic acid into lactic acid. It's often done during red wine fermentation to soften the acidity of the wine. Also known as secondary fermentation.

mesoclimate: Tiny area that has a different climate that those that surround it.

MOG: Material other than grapes.

must: Unfermented or fermenting grape juice that is becoming wine.

must pump: A hose and pumping device that is used to move must from one location to another or from the bottom of a tank to the top.

native (wild) yeast: The natural yeast found on the grapes. This is different from commercial yeasts which some winemakers add to start the fermentation process.

phenolic compounds: Pigments and tannins in wine.

phylloxera vastatrix (phylloxera): A louse that attacks the roots of the vine. It devastated vineyards in Europe and America in the 1800s. Rootstocks were developed that are resistant to the louse.

Pierce's disease: A disease caused by a bacterium spread by insects, primarily the blue-green sharpshooter. It can devastate a vineyard. The correct plants around the vineyard can prevent the insects from getting to the vines.

primary fermentation: The changing of grape juice into wine by converting grape sugar into ethyl alcohol and carbon dioxide.

prune: A way to shape the vine to insure the best possible fruit. There are several methods of pruning.

pump over: A process of taking the must or juice at the bottom of a tank and pouring or spraying it over the cap.

Rhône: A region in France noted for particular varietal grapes: Grenache, Mourvèdre, Cinsaut, Carignan, Syrah, Marsanne and Roussanne. Wines made from these grapes are frequently referred to as "Rhône varietal wines."

rootstock: Roots and bottom grape vine stem used as a basis for grafting clones. Biologists have developed rootstocks that are resistant to most diseases and insects that can affect grape vines.

sparge: Process of removing wine from barrels, putting it into tanks and then spraying with nitrogen to reduce the amount of oxygen in the wine. This reduces the need to use SO_2 to prevent Brettanomyces.

***sur lees* (on the lees):** A process of letting the lees, the insoluble material that drops out of wine, rest on the bottom of the tank or barrel during fermentation or aging. Some winemakers also stir the lees.

terroir: A term that changes its meaning depending on to who you talk to — whole books have been written about it.

uninoculated fermentation: The process of using native yeast to promote fermentation.

verasion: The moment when the grapes start to soften and change color, about eight weeks after bloom.

vinifera: The species of grape most often used for wine production.

vintage: The year the grapes for the wine were harvested

Suggested Reading

Hill, Kathleen and Gerald, *Monterey & Carmel, Eden by the Sea*, The Globe Pequot Press, Guilford, Connecticut, 2001.

Laube, James, *Wine Spectator's California Wine*, Wine Spectator Press, New York, 1995.

MacNeil, Karen, *The Wine Bible*, Workman Publishing, New York, 2001.

Reti, Ingrid, *Steinbeck Country Revisited*, Central Coast Press, San Luis Obispo, California, 2000.

Sullivan, Charles L., *A Companion to California Wine*, University of California Press, Berkeley, California, 1998.

_____, *Like Modern Edens, Winegrowing in Santa Clara Valley and Santa Cruz Mountains 1798–1981*, California History Center, Cupertino, CA 1982.

Woodward, W. Philip and Gregory S. Walter, *Chalone, A Journey on the Wine Frontier*, Carneros Press, 2000.

Young, Casey, *Mountain Vines, Mountain Wines: Exploring the wineries of the Santa Cruz Mountains*, Mountain Vines Publishing, Santa Cruz, California, 2003.

Winery Index

Tasting Notes

Tasting Notes

Tasting Notes

Learn more about unknown, but excellent wine regions!

Mountain Vines, Mountain Wines: Exploring the wineries of the Santa Cruz Mountains

Would you like to taste great wine, meet interesting winemakers, explore ancient forests and end your day with a great meal and entertainment? This book is your complete reference to more than 50 wineries in the Santa Cruz Mountains. Personalities, locations, and types of wines produced by each winery are combined with essential information about climate and history.
You will discover:

- Award-winning wines at niche wineries tucked into the mountains
- Events that give you access to winemakers without regular tasting hours
- Activities to combine with winery visits
- Geography and history that shaped Santa Cruz Mountains wineries
- The "story behind the bottle"

"This is an excellent historical background and up-to-date guide to the Santa Cruz Mountains. A concise and highly readable book, it gives the flavor of each of the wineries and the men and women who work with nature to produce their distinctive wines. A timely addition to the wine literature."

Paul Draper, Winemaker and CEO, Ridge Vineyards

Vineyards in the Sky

Meet Martin Ray, the vintner who in the 1930s began setting the stage for America's "Wine Revolution" by producing and marketing the first 100% varietal wines made from premier California grapes. Eleanor Ray provides a lifetime's worth of colorful tales and drama-packed events in this memoir-biography of Martin Ray, which reads like an epic novel. Books about wine are many, but a full-bodied portrait of a winegrower is a rarity - especially one that portrays a man so dynamic and utterly unique.

"This small-press publication is certainly worth tracking down. . . . It is a gripping memoir that reads like a 'major' novel. . . . Following Prohibition and under the tutelage of Paul Masson, Ray championed the varietal concept. His commitment to this ideal made him the gadfly of an industry that packaged inferior blends with misleading labels. Ray instead on producing pure varietal wines from premium grapes. It was this style of winemaking that would eventually bring California wines international recognition and adoration."

Anthony Dias Blue, on CBS and in a nationally syndicated wine column

Turn the page to purchase these books today!

QUICK ORDER

Telephone orders: Call 888-279-0122 toll free. Have your credit card ready.

email orders: orders@mountainvinespub.com

Postal Orders: Mountain Vines Publishing, P.O. Box 385, Aptos, CA 95001 USA

Telephone: 831-684-0522

Please send me the following books. I understand that I may return any of them for a full refund — for any reason, no questions asked.

Title	No. of Copies	Total Cost per Title
Mountain Vines, Mountain Wines — $24.95		
From the Highlands to the Sea — $24.95		
Vineyards in the Sky (biography of Martin Ray) — $21.95		
	Subtotal	
	Sales Tax *	
	Shipping	$4.10
	Total Cost	

Name: _____

Address: _____

City: _____

State: _____   Zip: _____

Telephone: _____

email address: _____

Please add me to your mailing list: _____

* Sales tax: Please add 8 % for products shipped to California addresses.

Shipping: $4.10 for priority mail shipping, no matter how many books you order!

Payment: Check or Money Order ___

Visa ___   MasterCard ___   AMEX ___   Discover ___

Card Number: _____

Name on card: _____ Exp. date: _____